MILLER'S

COLLECTING
PRINTS &
POSTERS

Miller's Collecting Prints & Posters
Janet Gleeson

First published in Great Britain in 1997 by Miller's
an imprint of Reed International Books Limited
Michelin House
81 Fulham Road
London SW3 6RB
and Auckland, Melbourne and Singapore

Executive Editor Alison Starling
Editor Elisabeth Faber
Executive Art Editor Vivienne Brar
Designers Nina Pickup and Jessica Caws
Picture Research Jenny Faithfull
Index Hilary Bird
Production Jilly Sitford
Special photography Ken Adlard, Ian Booth, Tim Ridley

© 1997 Reed International Books Limited

Set in Granjon and Helvetica Neue
Origination and printing by Mandarin Offset
Printed in Singapore

MILLER'S

COLLECTING

PRINTS &
POSTERS

Janet Gleeson

Special consultants: Richard Barclay, Stephen Maycock,
Louise Nason and Caroline Wiseman

The Author

Janet Gleeson is a journalist
who specializes in art and antiques.
She has been the auctions and
antiques writer for *House and
Garden* since 1988 and is a regular
contributor to *The Antique Collector*
and the *Sunday Times*. Janet was
General Editor of *Miller's Antiques
and Collectables*, *Collecting
Furniture* and *Collecting Pottery &
Porcelain*, all in the *Facts at Your
Fingertips* series.

Special Consultants

Richard Barclay joined Christie's in
1982, where he started the poster
department. He is Britain's leading
poster specialist.

Stephen Maycock is a consultant on
rock and pop at Sotheby's, London.
He is the author of *Miller's Rock and
Pop Memorabilia*.

Louise Nason has worked at
Christie's since 1992, and is their
expert on 18th- and 19th-century
English sporting, topographical
and decorative prints.

Caroline Wiseman, a qualified
barrister, is the director of Wiseman
Originals, specializing in 20th-century
original prints.

Contents

posters – you will come across that fall within the average collector's budget date from the 19th century onwards, so images from the last two centuries predominate. Many are realistically shown in the less than perfect condition in which you will find much art bought in sale rooms or galleries.

Values

What makes one image by a certain artist worth more than another by the same hand? A wide range of factors have to be weighed up when deciding value. The name of the artist has perhaps the most dramatic influence on prices. Fashion, technical skill and creative genius all play a part in making the work of certain artists more desirable than that of others.

Rarity has a huge bearing on the value of prints. Prints are by their nature multiples and, in general, the more versions of a certain print there are, the lower the price will be. Works by some very highly esteemed artists such as Hogarth were often reissued and the fact that there are so many later versions of his work has generally depressed prices.

The date and quality of the impression are equally important. Prints taken early in the life of a copper plate are more richly inked and detailed than later impressions and therefore more desirable.

Size and subject are also crucial to value. In general larger prints tend to cost more than smaller ones, but this rule of thumb can be instantly overturned by the subject of the painting. Fetching animals, pretty women, children, flower-filled gardens and charming cottages are all typical of commercially appealing subjects, for which demand and therefore prices are strong. Prints of less desirable subjects, such as gory battles, dead game or unattractive portraits, will nearly always be less valuable simply because they are more tricky to sell.

Provenance can greatly affect the price you pay for prints. An engraving that has belonged to an illustrious owner will always command a premium; this is partly why prints in important house sales always seem to sell so well. Condition is also crucial to value, but if you buy at auction you may be surprised to see that it is not always the prints in the most "perfect" condition that make the best prices. Dealers, who still dominate many print sales, nearly always avoid highly restored prints in case they are "trade" images that have languished in another dealer's stock and failed to sell. If you are tempted by a print or poster that

Introduction

One of the aims of this book is to highlight the accessibility of collecting prints. Whether you decide to specialize in antique prints or in modern original prints it is not difficult to pay far less than you would for a modern reproduction. Buying original prints can also have the added bonus of proving extremely beneficial financially. While a modern reproduction is devalued as soon as you buy it, provided you choose wisely, a print not only gives you the pleasure of ownership, but also stands a good chance of increasing in value over the years.

The prints and posters shown in this book have been chosen to reflect the type of material you can expect to see in sale rooms and galleries. The book has been divided into three areas. The first discusses the main printing techniques used to make both prints and posters. The second section deals with prints by subject, highlighting some of the most popular collecting areas. The third section is devoted to posters, arranged according to style and then subject matter. The vast majority of prints, and all of the looks the worse for wear, don't forget to take the cost of restoration into account before you buy.

Buying & selling

Buying an authentic item is obviously a major concern for any novice collector. The best way to avoid pitfalls is to buy from reputable sources, such as from a dealer who belongs to a recognized trade association (see p152), from a vetted fair or from a reputable auction house. Much expertise is based on an instinctive reaction to the appearance of a print. Teaching yourself to recognize authentic prints of good quality is essential not only to avoid fakes, but also to spot bargains. Visit dealers, auction rooms and museums to train your eye to recognize quality and authenticity. Auction house experts and dealers will usually be only too willing to help and advise you.

Buying from a dealer

Buying from a dealer who is a member of a trade association gives you several important safeguards. In order to have joined the association, a dealer will have had his stock assessed and found to be of good quality, and will also have shown that he has a sound knowledge of his subject. When buying a print from a dealer ensure you are given a full written receipt, stating the price, date and a full description of the print, including artist, technique, date and subject.

Fairs

Fairs are one of the most rapidly growing methods of buying, and are particularly useful to novice buyers in providing a selection of dealers under one roof allowing you to compare prices and stock. They will also enable you to make contact with dealers from other parts of the country or from abroad. Most of the larger fairs are "vetted", meaning that all the stock has been scrutinized by a panel of experts to ensure authenticity. Prints may be found at most general antiques fairs and also specialist events (see p154).

Auctions

All of the large auction houses hold regular sales of antique and modern prints and smaller sale rooms often offer them in general picture auctions. Auctions provide an ideal opportunity for collectors to get hands-on experience of looking at and examining prints, and are frequently a great source of bargains. While in dealers' galleries prints are usually sold framed or mounted, many prints seen in sale rooms will be unframed in "folio" lots or stuck into old albums. Buying prints unframed is usually a less expensive way of starting a collection. The prints on offer in a sale room will be described in a catalogue of the sale, and numbered in the order they will be sold. The catalogue will usually tell you some or all of the following: the name of the artist, the name of the subject, the printing method, the date of publication, the publisher, size and estimated price. Most descriptions also include some reference to the condition of the image and to the quality of the impression. Bear in mind that on top of the hammer price you will have to pay the auctioneer's commission and VAT on the commission.

Price guides

The values given in this book are intended only as a rough guide and (with the exception of modern original prints, where dealers' prices are given) are based on auction house prices. Ultimately at auction the value of any work of art is what two or more people are willing to pay for it. If you compare the price of similar prints at a dealer's you may find them slightly higher. This is because while at auction you are buying "wholesale", the dealer has to make a profit to survive. In many cases the dealer may also have had the print restored, researched it and mounted or framed it. The price will reflect this.

Finally, remember to buy only what you like, and the best that you can afford. It is nearly always better in the long run to buy one really good picture than three or four indifferent ones.

Understanding the print line

Prints often contain useful information that typically appears immediately underneath the image or as part of a "print line". Generally the artist's name (after whom the print may have been made) was positioned on the left-hand side, the publisher's name in the middle, and the printmaker's name on the right. Names are usually preceded by Latin terms describing the different tasks involved in making the print, including drawing, engraving or publishing, which are often abbreviated. The most commonly seen terms and abbreviations are listed here:

Delineavit (del., delin.) – "drew this" – refers to the name of the artist

Execudit (ex., excud.) – "published this" – refers to the publisher

Fecit (f., fec., or fac.) – "made this" – refers to the name of the printmaker

Impressit (imp.) – "printed this" – refers to the name of the printmaker

Invenit (inv.) – "designed this" – refers to the artist

Lithog. – refers to the artist or the lithographer

Pinxit – "painted this" – refers to the artist

Sculpsit (sc., sculp.) – "engraved this" – refers to the name of the printmaker

The Print

Margin

Artist's name

Title

ROSS CASTLE *on the Island of Ro*

T. Walmsley Pinx.

Published, as the Act directs, by T. Walmsley, N.º 5.

◄ **After Thomas Sotelle Roberts**
Ross Castle, a coloured aquatint by S.
Alken, first published 1795–6. **£150–250**

Engraver's name

Publisher

Wood Cutting

❶ The initial design is cut into the block of wood with a knife. The image can then be refined and finished using other tools such as a gouge (shown here), which creates v-shaped grooves.

❷ The block is inked with a roller. The ink must be of a viscous consistency so that it only covers the areas that have not been cut away and does not run into the hollows. It is these uncut areas that appear as solid blocks of colour in the final print.

❸ The inked block is placed on the press. The small black tabs at the edge of the wood block are registration tabs. These allow the printmaker to remove the block and replace it in exactly the same place on the press. This is especially useful when printing woodcuts in several colours.

❹ "Pulling" the print. The printmaker pulls the lever of the manual press, thus exerting gentle pressure on the block. Presses such as this example, which dates from the second half of the 19th century, are still very much in use today.

❺ The frame of the press is lifted up and the paper is peeled off the wood block. Because the pressure needed to print woodcuts is light in comparison to that needed for etchings, the paper is not generally left with a platemark.

❻ The finished woodcut. (For further discussion of this technique see pp14–15.)

Etching

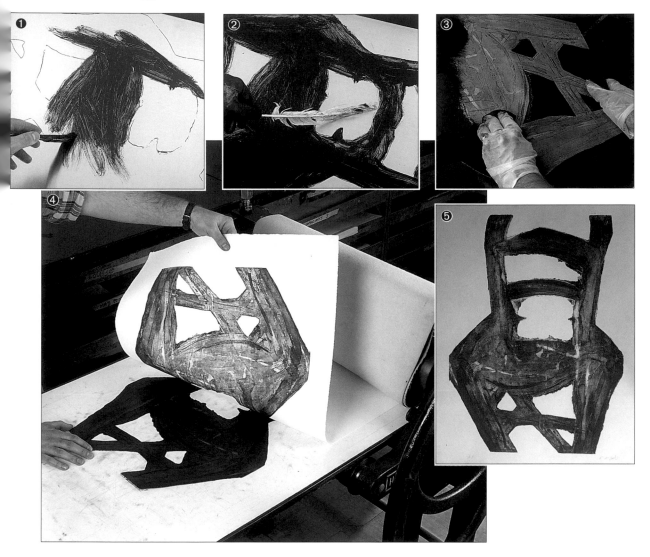

❶ The shape of the image is painted on a metal plate with an acid-resistant varnish, or "ground". In this example the ground has been painted on so that the resulting image will resemble brush strokes. The ground can also be scratched into using a burin, to achieve delicate lines.

❷ The metal plate is immersed in an acid bath. The acid bites into all areas of the metal not covered with the resistant varnish. The acid causes gas bubbles to form, and these must be brushed away with a feather to prevent the acid from biting unevenly. The plate is then rinsed off to stop the process. Areas that are sufficiently etched can be masked with the acid-resistant substance, known as "stopping out", and the plate can then be placed in the acid again so that other areas can be more deeply etched.

❸ Once the acid etching is complete, the ground is cleaned off the plate and then the ink is applied. Because etching is a more delicate method than wood cutting, the inking is done by wiping the plate by hand. On traditional etchings the ink on the surface is wiped away leaving ink only in the grooves. Here a reverse surface printing technique is used.

❹ The inked plate is covered with dampened paper and slowly passed through a roller press. Once pressed, the paper is peeled off the plate (illustrated here). Intaglio processes such as etching and engraving require much more pressure than relief methods, making the roller press more suitable.

❺ The finished etching. (For further discussion of this technique see pp28–9.)

Lithography

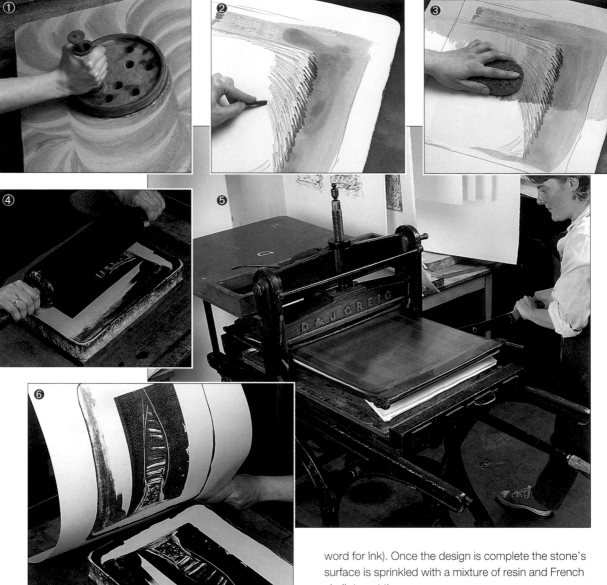

word for ínk). Once the design is complete the stone's surface is sprinkled with a mixture of resin and French chalk to set the grease.

❸ Liquid gum is sponged over the stone. This process helps the stone absorb the grease and sets the image. The surface is then cleaned with spirit.

❶ The lithographic stone is prepared – a process known as "levigating" – by covering its surface in water and grinding it with a gritty substance using regular rotating motions. This leaves the stone's porous surface clean and free of any grease left over from previous use.

❹ The stone is wetted and inked with a roller. The greasy ink only "takes" on the greased areas, but is repelled by the wet ungreased areas.

❺ Paper is laid over the stone and they are passed through a roller press.

❷ The design is drawn on the stone with a greasy crayon. Designs can also be painted on using a brush dipped in a solution called "tusche" (from the German

❻ The finished lithograph is lifted off the stone. (For further discussion see pp36–7).

Screen Printing

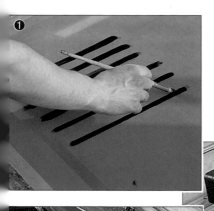

began to be used in the 1990s for health reasons, dry much faster than the traditional oil-based inks, and so the printing must be done as soon as the screen has been inked.

❶ A design is painted onto the screen with an ink-resistant masking varnish. Areas can also be masked using stencils, a method well-suited to the bold abstract designs with which screen printing is associated. Light-sensitive substances can also be used to create photographic images on the mesh, a technique that was most famously used in Pop Art. Designs painted on the screen are negative rather than positive.

❷ Coloured ink is poured along the edge of the screen. A blade, known as a "squeegee", is then wiped across the screen to evenly distribute the ink. This is known as "flooding". Water-based inks, which

❸ The paper to receive the print is placed under the screen and the squeegee is wiped back across it, pressing the ink through onto the paper.

❹ The screen is lifted up to reveal the printed paper. The areas that have been masked on the screen have remained blank on the paper. This process will then be repeated using different coloured inks and masking different areas of the screen, so that a multi-coloured, multi-layered design is gradually built up on one piece of paper.

❺ The finished screenprint. (For further discussion of this technique see pp46–7.)

Relief Printing

The evolution of printing: from the earliest medieval woodcuts to the lino cuts of the 20th century

▲ **George Claude Leon Underwood**
Underwood is one of the leading wood engravers of the 1920s.
This scene of *The Nativity* is particularly affordable. **£20–30**

Relief printing encompasses woodcutting (the oldest printing method) and wood engraving. Other printing methods where the image to be printed stands proud from the background, and is formed by inking the surface of the block, are also forms of relief printing. These methods use a reverse process from intaglio printing (see p22), where the image is made by grooves cut into the surface, and the surface itself provides the white areas.

Woodcuts were made by drawing an image on to the smoothed surface of a plank of wood on which the grain runs parallel to the cut. The woods used varied, but tended to be fairly soft timbers such as sycamore, cherry and pear. The white areas of the design were gouged out and cut away with a knife leaving only the areas to be printed black standing in relief, an astonishing feat when you look at the fineness of line achieved in some 16th-century woodcuts. Once the block was carved, ink was applied to the surface using a dabber

or a roller. The ink had to be fairly viscous in order to stay only on the surface and not run into the hollow white areas. A piece of paper was then laid on the block and gentle pressure applied by hand or with a press to transfer the image (see p10).

This simple but laborious printing method gives woodcuts a distinctive appearance. The lines are comparatively heavy, and often look uneven in width when examined closely. Unlike an intaglio print there is no plate mark because relatively little pressure is applied during the printing process, and the surface of the print feels flat. Because the blocks were cut parallel to the grain, curved shapes had to be cut across the fibres of the wood and therefore often look rather angular. In large black areas the grain is sometimes visible. Woodcutting is best suited to creating bold, linear images, but less suited to portraying tone and fine details.

The chiaroscuro woodcut which evolved in Italy and Germany in the 16th century simulated the effect of a wash drawing by

▼ John Baptist Jackson
Jackson specialized in chiaroscuro woodcuts after the old masters producing images using up to six separate blocks. This is one of 8 plates from a full set of 24 showing masterpieces by Italian artists, including Titian, Veronese and other Venetian artists. This example is after a painting by Tintoretto. **£400–600** for set of 8

reproducing tones as well as line. Chiaroscuro woodcuts use the same method as woodcuts but the image was printed in up to three shades: usually mustard, brown and black or shades of green, with a different block being used for each shade and the white of the paper providing the highlights. Colour woodcuts were also made during the 19th century for book illustrations using the same technique.

Wood engraving was an 18th-century development of woodcutting. Wood engravings were made by using a block of a hard, finely grained wood – traditionally boxwood – that was cut across at right angles to the grain and highly polished. The image was incised into the wood using a type of burin (engraver's tool) and the technique allowed the printmaker to achieve far more detail than was possible using the woodcutting method. This printing method usually created a white line on a black background, because the line drawn by the printmaker was incised into the surface and therefore did not get inked during printing (although there are also black line wood engravings). Since the block was cut across, the grain of the wood did not hamper the design and wood engraving therefore allowed far more delicate and curvilinear designs.

Both woodcuts and wood engravings enjoyed a revival of popularity in the late 19th and early 20th centuries when artists became interested in exploring traditional printmaking techniques and developing new methods of their own. Their experimentation and the emergence of new materials led also to lino cutting. When warmed, lino is particularly pliable and the surface could be gouged away to create an image in relief which was then inked in the same way as woodcuts. The smooth, soft textureless surface of the man-made material provided printmakers with a far more versatile substance with which to work and resulted in some of the most varied and visually arresting relief prints ever made.

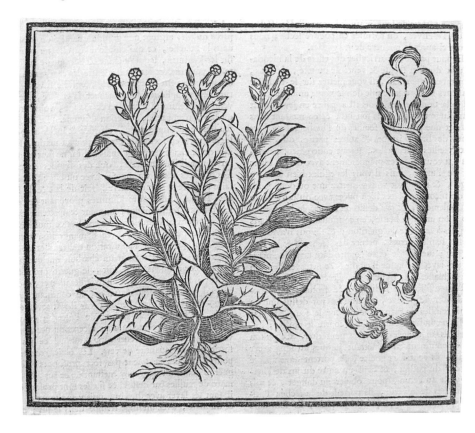

◀ **French School**
A 16th-century woodcut from a herbal. The text on the back shows that this has been taken from a book and the price of such individual studies is very affordable. **£20–40**

▶ **The Trojan Horse**
A typical 16th-century European woodcut illustrating a story from classical antiquity and probably taken from a book. Despite its age it is of comparatively low value. **£30–50**

Woodcuts

Woodcuts were the earliest method of relief printing and probably originated in China where they are known to have been in use c. 800AD. In Europe and the Middle East the method was chiefly used to print textiles until the 15th century, by which time small woodcuts were also used for book illustration, playing cards and small religious illustrations – the latter, often produced in monasteries, were possibly intended as mementoes of a pilgrimage. Throughout the 16th century woodcuts continued to evolve chiefly as a method of book illustration because the wood blocks could be made to the same thickness as fixed type, and text and image printed together. In contrast, illustrations made with intaglio printing methods, although more detailed and refined, had to be printed separately and inserted into the book, a process which made these methods far more expensive for book illustration.

Well-known early makers of woodcuts include Martin Schongauer, a Colmar artist who like Dürer (the most accomplished early printmaker of woodcuts) was the son of a goldsmith; Lucas Cranach the Elder, Hans Brosamer, Hans Baldung, Hans Sebald Beham and Urs Graf were also masters of the art. Most artists concentrated on copying paintings by other artists, many of them signing only with their initials which appear in the image. If their full names remain unidentified they may be catalogued by their monogram.

Woodcuts gradually waned in popularity and quality in the 17th century as intaglio techniques evolved although they continued to be used for book illustrations in herbals and for printing popular broadsheets. However, towards the end of the 19th century and early 20th century, woodcuts enjoyed a huge revival of interest. On the Continent leading avant-garde artists such as Gaugin, Braque, Munch, Kandinsky, Vlaminck and Max Pechstein began exploiting the forceful impact that could be achieved using this method. Their woodcuts are highly stylized and emphatically primitive. Some artists, mainly German Expressionists, experimented by incorporating the grain of the wood in the design, or by scoring the flat surface of the wood to create additional texture and visual interest. In England the printmaking revival was started by William Morris, the founder of the Kelmscott Press which produced books illustrated by traditional techniques. During the early years of the 20th century a new generation of young artists, such as

Collecting
Albrecht Dürer

▲ **Albrecht Dürer**
The Expulsion from Paradise, woodcut from the *Small Passion*, first of a state of two, a good impression on watermarked paper (5 x 4in/126 x 98mm). **£700–900**

Roger Fry, Edward Wadsworth, Paul Nash, Edward Bawden, Eric Ravilious, Leon Underwood and Charles Hazelwood Shannon, were among a number of artists to revive the art of woodcutting and wood engraving (see pp18–19) using woodcutting to portray modern industrial subjects as well as more traditionally decorative subjects.

In general, woodcuts are less numerous than many of the more popular forms of intaglio prints such as engravings and etchings, although they have survived in surprising quantities. Old master woodcuts have long been considered collectable and are often found trimmed and pasted into albums, a factor which can make identification difficult. Early unidentified examples may be dated by the paper, which should be pulpy and uneven in texture. The most valuable woodcuts are good impressions in good condition by known old master printmakers, or those by famous late 19th–early 20th-century artists. The works of German Expressionist artists command particularly high sums. All 20th-century woodcuts should be signed in pencil by the artist, and usually numbered to indicate the length of the edition. Unsigned illustrations by modern artists taken from books are far less valuable.

One of the most famous and highly skilled makers of woodcuts was Albrecht Dürer, who introduced an incredible level of sophistication to the technique. Dürer's woodcuts were often unusually large and attempted to create some of the subtlety of an oil painting by representing light and shade with delicate lines carved with incredible finesse. Dürer's fame and influence in northern Europe was largely based on his graphic output; he was also an accomplished engraver (see p24).

He produced several series of woodcuts including the *Apocalypse* (1498), the first book to be printed and published by the artist; *The Great Passion* (1498–1510); *The Little Passion* (1509–11); the *Life of the Virgin* (1501–11); and various single prints. Dürer's woodcuts were republished several times within his lifetime, and for over a century after his death. As a result, examples of his work appear regularly in sales of old master prints. As the blocks deteriorated changes were made that can help with dating. Value can be greatly affected by the rarity of the state (see p6) and the date of the edition as well as by the usual criteria of quality of impression, and condition. Good early woodcuts can fetch £15,000–20,000, while less rare subjects start at around £400.

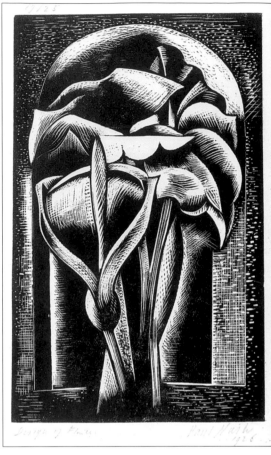

▲ **Charles Frederick Tunnicliffe**
The Black Bull, a wood engraving
with margins signed and
numbered 26/50 in pencil, on
wove paper. Tunnicliffe specialized
in birds and animal subjects and
his work is much sought after.
Fine examples such as this sell
for **£600–800**.

Wood Engraving

The potential of wood engraving was first developed by Thomas Bewick in the 18th century. A native of Newcastle, Bewick served his apprenticeship as an engraver on copper under Ralph Beilby. Bewick discovered that by using a highly polished, finely grained wood block cut across the grain he could incise it using similar tools to those of a metal engraver. The technique allowed greater versatility than woodcutting. Tone could be represented by fine cross hatching or lines, while depth could be suggested by slightly lowering the background so that these areas printed grey. Bewick was a keen observer of the countryside around him and many of his most accomplished works are based on sketches and watercolours of animals and birds drawn from life. His wood engravings range from small vignettes, for which he is best known, to larger compositions such as *The Chillingham Bull*, one of his most sought-after wood engravings. Much of his work was made to illustrate educational books such as *A General History of Quadrupeds* and *A History of British Birds* and, apart from a few outstanding exceptions, prints taken from books are usually sold in multi-lots for modest sums.

During the 19th century wood engraving was extensively used as a method of illustrating magazines such as the *Illustrated London News* and *Punch*. Artists themselves did not usually engrave the wood; their designs were drawn on the block and transferred into engravings by specialist craftsmen, and in the days before mechanical printing processes even photographs could be reproduced in this way. These can generally be obtained for low sums.

By the early decades of the 20th century photo-mechanical printing processes had superseded wood engraving as the most efficient way of reproducing illustrations but wood engraving was increasingly exploited by artist printmakers who took part in the general revival of printmaking techniques. Artists became involved both in the design of the image as well as its transferral into an engraving on wood and this gave the images great individuality and artistic appeal. Leading wood engravers of the turn of the century include Charles

◄ **Paul Nash**
Design of Flowers, by one of the leading wood engravers of the early 20th century. This example is signed, dated, titled and numbered in pencil as are most collectable 20th-century prints. **£300–400**

◄ ▲ **Douglas Percy Bliss**
Wood engravings entitled *The Gamekeeper* and *The Catch* signed and dated 1925 in pencil on simili-japan paper. The subject matter would appeal to collectors of angling and sporting prints as well as general print collectors and would increase the value. **£200–400** (for the pair)

Ricketts and Charles Hazelwood Shannon. Ricketts assumed the running of the Vale Press in Chelsea and was responsible for publishing *The Dial*, an influential magazine featuring his own work and that of other printmakers in the circle such as Thomas Sturge Moore and Lucien Pissarro. Both Ricketts and Shannon specialized in highly decorative designs that owe a debt to the flowing wood engravings of William Morris. Shannon's figurative subject matter is often circular in shape (see p21). His work has enjoyed a revival of interest in recent years and prices have risen considerably. Prints should be signed in pencil, either with the initials CS or in full.

Another leading 20th-century wood engraver was Eric Gill. Gill studied at the Central School of Art in London and is also known as a calligrapher and sculptor – among his best-known sculptures are the 14 stone Stations of the Cross in Westminster Cathedral, London. He was also a keen experimenter with printing techniques and made woodcuts (see illustration on p6) and black line

wood engravings by treating the block in the same way as a copper plate and printing from them in intaglio. At Ditchling in Sussex, Gill founded a lay order of artists in 1907.

Gill's work is characterized by its strong use of line and pattern. Figurative subject matter, whether of an erotic, religious or moral theme, dominates much of his printed output. From 1924 he began illustrating books published by the Golden Cockerel Press, run by Robert Gibbings with whom he helped found the Society of Wood Engravers. Much of his work was made as book illustrations which were also published in limited editions. Among the other founder members of the society were Edward Gordon Craig, John Nash and Noel Rooke.

Although wood engravings are generally finer in appearance than woodcuts, the two can be difficult to tell apart, since some artists deliberately tried to emulate woodcuts while using the wood engraving method. Value is not affected by the technique, however; the artist and the quality of the image are far more important.

▶ **Cyril Power**
Cyril Power produced strong designs using
lino cutting. This composition is entitled
Lifts and typically focuses on a futuristic
theme. **£1,000–2,000**

▲ **Michael Rothenstein**
Cockerel Turning Round (1956–7) shows the variety
of texture that can be achieved using chiaroscuro. It
is signed and numbered 7/50 in pencil. **£150–250**

Chiaroscuro, Colour Woodcuts, Lino Cuts

The chiaroscuro woodcut, an astonishingly sophisticated development of the woodcutting technique, became popular in Italy and northern Europe in the 16th century. The printing method allowed printmakers to simulate the effect of pen and wash drawings that were popular with collectors at the time, and many copies of wash drawings by celebrated painters such as Raphael and Parmigianino were made into prints by Ugo da Carpi and Antonio da Trento. In general northern European chiaroscuro woodcuts, by artists such as Hendrick Goltzius tend to be more linear, while those made by Italian artists are more tonal. Other printmakers were Bartolommeo Coriolano who made prints after Guido Reni, and Andrea Andreani whose prints were made after painings by Mantegna and other less well-known artists. Chiaroscuro woodcuts of old master paintings remained popular in the 18th century and specialists include Count Antonio Maria Zanetti, and John Baptist Jackson.

Colour woodcuts were made using a technique similar to that used for chiaroscuro woodcuts. Separate blocks were cut, each block representing a different colour used in the design. Many designs also had a black outline that would be printed first and provide the key block against which the various colours would be positioned. The technique achieved unrivalled sophistication in Japan in the 18th century, where numerous blocks were used to create images of great subtlety, and additional surface pattern and texture was sometimes created by embossing parts of the print by pressing it with blocks carved with pattern but not inked. Japanese woodblocks began to reach Europe in the 19th century and had a profound impact on many of the leading artists of the day.

Colour woodcuts became a popular method of book illustration during the 19th century and were also explored by many European and British artists in the early 20th century. One of the most notable British artists to develop the technique was William Nicholson who made colour woodcuts often limited in tone to shades of green. His best-known image, a portrait of Queen Victoria in 1897, the year of her Diamond Jubilee, led to a series of 12 portraits of prominent figures such as the Prince of Wales and Sarah Bernhardt. Much of the work produced by

▼ **Charles Hazelwood Shannon**
Fruit picking, Winter, one of a set of 12 chiaroscuro woodcuts made 1903–4 showing Shannon's skill in using shape, colour and form to create a strong surface pattern. The set sold for **£550**.

▲ **Sybil Andrews**
Golgotha exhibits a typically striking design by this artist who specialized in lino cuts. The image is printed on japan tissue and inscribed "No T.P." **£200–300**

Nicholson was published both as woodcuts in limited numbers and in large editions of lithographs, which are far less valuable.

During the 20th century lino cuts became one of the most popular methods of colour relief printing. Artists favoured the lino cut method because the material was soft, pliable, easy to work with and inexpensive. In mainland Europe many well-known artists experimented with the technique. Henri Matisse used lino cuts to illustrate Montherlant's *Pasiphaë* in 1944, in which he exploited the softness of the material by creating images by defining them with fine white lines set against a black background. The prolific print-maker Pablo Picasso produced a famous series of lino cuts when in 1958 he moved away from the studios of Paris and settled in the South of France. Frustrated by the difficulties of dispatching lithographic proofs to Paris he was determined to experiment with this more versatile printing method. Picasso's lino cuts are characterized by rich colour and bold decorative forms. His technique was unusual in that most of the prints were made from a single block, rather than different ones for each colour. After each colour was printed part of the design was removed before the next was printed.

In England in 1913–15 the French sculptor and designer Henri Gaudier-Brzeska, a founder member of the Vorticists, made striking lino cuts reflecting his interest in abstraction and primitive art. Lino cutting became increasingly popular in the 1920s and 1930s. Among the leading British exponents of the form are Sybil Andrews and her husband Cyril Power. Andrews is best known for her dramatically coloured rustic scenes in which tones such as black, green, ochre and orange often predominate. Cyril Power's work is often futuristic in its themes, but both artists bring to the technique a strong sense of pattern and movement. Their work is often printed on thin tissue paper and, as if to underline the hand-made quality of the printing technique, the ink has a distinctive smudgy appearance especially around the margins. Prints have often been mounted onto card and collectors should check the corners for evidence of tearing as this will reduce the value of the print. Andrews' lino cuts were usually made in series of 50 or 60. Prices for Power's work are usually higher than for Andrews'.

Intaglio Printing

From early line engravings, stipple engraving and etching to mezzotints and aquatints

NORTH FRONT OF THE LIBRARY OF CHRIST CHURCH COLLEGE

▲ Subjects
Although there are no publishing details on this aquatint because the margins have been trimmed, its subject matter – a view of Christ Church Library – make it a sought-after print. Oxford, London and Continental scenes are always in high demand. **£50–60** upwards

Intaglio is an Italian word which means engraving, and of the three main printing groups intaglio printing has given rise to the largest and most diverse range of printing techniques including engraving, stipple engraving, etching, drypoint, mezzotint and aquatints.

Intaglio printing involves cutting or incising an image into a metal plate using various methods (described in more detail on the following pages); the plate is then usually warmed and ink is applied using a roller and a dabber. The use of heat reduces the viscosity of the ink and helps it to permeate into the incisions. The surface of the plate is then lightly wiped clean, leaving ink only in the grooves. After soaking the paper in a bath of water to make it more malleable it is placed on top of the plate and a layer of felt padding placed on top. Paper and plate are then passed through a rolling press, which was traditionally operated with a winding handle. The pressure of the rollers forces the soft wet paper into the grooves of the plate and the ink thus transferred. Once it has passed through the rollers the print is then carefully lifted off the plate and dried and the plate reinked and wiped before printing again. The pressure to which the print is subjected during the printing process creates a distinctive line around the edge of the plate, known as the plate mark, and when examined closely the lines forming the image can often be seen to be slightly raised or embossed. Most of the intaglio prints made before the 19th century were produced on copper plates.

◀ **Edmund Blampied**
Sunday Morning Bathers – drypoint, 1920, signed in pencil. Blampied capitalizes on the sketchiness of drypoint in this atmospheric equestrian subject. **£600–800**

▲ **Alfred Charles Stanley Anderson**
The Thatcher exemplifies the 20th-century resurgence of interest in engraving. This is a signed, titled and inscribed edition of 60 prints. The paper's uneven edge is known as a "deckle edge". **£300–400**

◀ **After William Redmore Bigg**
Saturday Morning, or *The Cottagers' Merchandise*, one of a pair of stipple engravings part-printed in colour by William Nutter, sold recently for **£400** (see p53 for the other half of the pair).

Copper is a relatively soft metal and as the plate was used the surface of the metal and finer details were gradually worn away. For this reason earlier impressions, which are usually identifiable by their richness and the fine definition of the image, are far more desirable than later ones.

All forms of intaglio prints use the same method to transfer the image to the paper though in each case the image is formed in a slightly different way. In engraving the artist incises directly onto the plate using a cutting instrument called a burin. In etching the acid is used to create the incised image and drypoint and soft ground etchings are variations on the technique. All these methods create essentially linear images, however, and this limitation was overcome by two other important intaglio printing methods which allowed the artist to create a more tonal picture. Mezzotints became popular in the 17th century for reproducing the rich chiaroscuro (light and shade) of oil painting. Similarly in the 18th century aquatints were found to be effective for reproducing the soft appearance of watercolours.

All types of intaglio print would originally have had a plate mark surrounded by margins and most also have a print line underneath showing the publisher, the artist and the engraver. If the print has been trimmed to the plate mark and the print line is missing this will invariably reduce the desirability of the image, although value also depends greatly on the richness of the impression, the subject matter and the rarity.

▼ **Victorian steel engravings**
A typical, late 19th-century steel engraving from a book. Often the engraver's name does not appear on the image. Prints of this type have little value unless the subject is particularly interesting. **£5–10**

▲ ▶ **Hendrick Goltzius**
This classical subject was engraved by one of the leading old masters, Hendrick Goltzius. The detail shows the collector's mark of Thomas Lawrence, which adds to the desirability of the engraving. **£100–200**

Engraving

Engravings were traditionally made on a copper or steel plate using a cutting tool known as a burin which gouged out a V-shaped section of metal. The design was created by lines of varying thickness and depth – the deeper the furrow, the wider and blacker the line will print. Areas of tone and shadow were created by cross hatching or by series of fine lines. By varying the angle of the burin the engraver could also control and vary the width of a continuous line.

One of the distinctive characteristics of an engraving is that lines terminate in a point, created by the V-shape of the burin. Line engravings are the earliest type of intaglio prints and are thought to have been developed in the mid-15th century in Europe by goldsmiths who were highly skilled at decorating metal with engraved designs.

The engraving technique lends itself to a rather linear, formal style of drawing. Figure subjects whether religious, mythological, genre or portraits predominate, although the technique was also used for architectural and scientific drawings where accuracy was more important than artistic expression. The earliest identified engraver was Martin Schongauer, a German painter and printmaker based in Colmar who made numerous fine extraordinarily detailed engravings of religious subjects.

Along with Schongauer Albrecht Dürer was the most influential engraver in northern Europe throughout the 15th and early 16th centuries (see p. 17), creating incredibly subtle effects of light and shade and tone through his gradation of line. Other famous early engravers include Marcantonio Raimondi who made engravings after Raphael, and Lucas van Leyden, and engraved genre scenes and mythological subjects. Many early printmakers are anonymous or signed with a monogram and are known only by their initials. In the following centuries engravings were often used as a way of reproducing paintings. One of the most prolific engravers was the Dutch artist Hendrick Goltzius. Goltzius' early work in the Mannerist tradition gave way to classical compositions later in his life, following his visit to Rome. He is especially renowned for his technical proficiency and a feature of his engravings is their distinctive continual lines of variable thickness achieved by altering the angle of the burin on the copper plate.

In England, engraving started in the mid-16th century and among the most notable early examples were maps produced by Saxton, Morden and Speed (see pp62–3). Many early English engravings were made by Flemish artists and portraits formed the majority of their output throughout the 17th

The thing that hath been it is that which shall be and that which is done is that which shall be done. To every thing there is a season and a time to every purpose under the heaven. Ecclesiastes

▶ *Arrested For Debt*
A single plate from a set of eight from Hogarth's series *The Rake's Progress*. Hogarth's most popular prints were reprinted throughout the 18th century. Early impressions usually cost **£30–100**, later ones such as this under £30.

Collecting
William Hogarth

IS ARRESTED GOING TO COURT.

One of the most prolific English engravers, William Hogarth trained as an engraver in silver and began his professional career as a copper engraver of book illustrations. In the 1730s, having studied painting under Sir James Thornhill whose daughter he later married, he began a series of satirical scenes of English life which related a story in installments. The first, called *The Harlot's Progress*, contained six scenes; this was followed by *The Rake's Progress* and *Marriage à la Mode*. The series, reproduced as engravings by Hogarth and other artists, enjoyed huge success and were much copied, so much so that Hogarth lobbied for a copyright law, which was passed in 1735. The law stipulated that all prints should bear the name of the publisher and date of issue of the print. Hogarth held back the publication of *The Rake's Progress* until after the act was passed, but despite this precaution, by the time it was printed pirated copies were already flooding the market.

Hogarth's prints have been extensively republished and reprinted and identification can provide numerous pitfalls for the novice collector. Bound sets were issued by Hogarth himself; and as the 14-year copyright expired more copies were made, until in 1767 Hogarth's widow was granted a copyright extension of 20 years. When she died the plates were reissued by the publisher Boydell & Boydell who also had new plates made from Hogarth's designs, including mezzotints of *Marriage à la Mode* by Richard Earlom (pub. 1795). During the 19th century the plates continued to be used and these later versions have very little value as collectable prints. The flood of reprints has dramatically affected the value of Hogarth engravings; even early versions can be bought at auction for modest sums.

century. One of the most important native 17th-century engravers was William Faithorne, a royalist supporter in the English Civil War, who probably perfected his art working with Robert Nanteuil, a celebrated French engraver, while he lived in exile in France during Cromwell's rule. Faithorne returned to England in 1650 after the restoration of the monarchy and made engravings after all the leading portraitists of the day including van Dyck, Dobson and Lely and also engraved from his own life drawings.

During the early 18th century engraving, often used in conjunction with etching, was a popular printing technique for reproducing architectural subjects. One of the most celebrated English publications was *Vitruvius Britannicus* by Colen Campbell, a folio containing engravings of designs for classically inspired architecture (see p56). Later in the 18th century line engraving began to become less popular as more versatile printing techniques were developed. By the mid-19th century steel plates were being used for engraving. Steel was far more durable than copper so the number of print impressions that could be produced increased. Steel engravings have a harsher appearance and more precise lines and are generally far less desirable than those made from copper plates.

▲ After Angelica Kauffmann
Blind Man's Buff, a typical 18th-century decorative stipple engraving printed in sepia by P. W. Tomkins and F. Bartolozzi, published 1783.
£150–250

▶ After Giovanni Battista Cipriani
Stipple engraving of a muse part-printed in colour by Francesco Bartolozzi, the leading stipple engraver of the 18th century. The attractive *verre églomisé* frame also adds to its appeal.
£100–200

◀ Stipple engraving
The detail shows the distinctive series of dots and short etched lines found in stipple engravings, and the use of printed and hand colouring. Here the green and brown are printed while the cheeks, lips and other details are hand-coloured.

Stipple & Crayon Manner Engraving

Stipple engraving was an intaglio printing method that allowed the artist to represent subtle gradations of tone by building up the composition using a series of tiny dots and lines. The method enjoyed a heyday of popularity from the mid-18th century until the early decades of the 19th century when it was much used for decorative and genre subjects after paintings by well-known artists.

The technique varied, but usually involved preparing a copper plate by coating it with an acid-resistant ground, in the same way as etching (see pp28–9). The engraver outlined the design with a series of dots and then exposed the plate to acid. When the design was bitten into the plate, the ground was removed and the image worked up with special roulettes (see p27), burins and needles to create the distinctive pitted effect.

Stipple engravings were printed using the same basic method as other forms of intaglio print, and a plate mark would originally have been visible. Some were printed with the usual black ink; many were printed in reddish sepia tones, which added to the softness of the overall impression; while more expensive stipples were part-printed in colour. This time-consuming method involved inking the plate with colours in between each printing. Usually no more than two shades were used (typically brown and blue) and the other colours and fine details were added by hand after printing. Colour printing in this method is known as *à la poupée* and, because each plate was separately coloured, no two prints will be exactly alike.

Stipple engraving was mainly practised by printmakers in England but its most famous exponent was a Florentine, Francesco Bartolozzi. Bartolozzi built up a reputation in Florence for engravings after old master paintings and came to England in the mid-18th century to make copies of Guercino drawings in the Royal Collection. He was appointed engraver to George III in 1764 and remained in England for nearly four decades. Bartolozzi's stipple engravings typically feature attractive cupids and languid classical maidens, or genre scenes with a sentimental message and are usually based on paintings by Angelica Kauffmann, Giovanni Battista Cipriani or Francis Wheatley.

► ▼ **After François Boucher**
Young Girl with a Dog and *Le Sommeil de Vénus*, two crayon manner etchings by Giles Antoine Demarteau. The technique was much used in France to simulate chalk drawings. **£200–300** the pair

Bartolozzi had many pupils who he trained up including William Nutter, Edmund Scott, Robert Samuel Marcand, P. W. Tomkins and Jean Marie Delatre, who became his principal assistant. Other leading exponents include François Davide Soiren, John Raphael Smith (who is also known for his mezzotints), Thomas Ryder and William Wynn Ryland – who was subsequently hanged for engraving forged banknotes.

Stipple engravings have generally enjoyed a revival of interest recently and prices have risen as a result. Prices depend heavily on the decorativeness of the subject and the quality of the impression. As with other forms of prints, the longer the plate is used the less well-defined the image becomes. As details become lost heavier colouring is often used to compensate and the best stipple engravings should look crisp and clear.

Stipple engravings have long been considered worthy of framing and displaying on a wall and many are found in old, often highly decorative, frames. Circular and oval shapes were particularly popular in the 18th and early 19th centuries and

prints in their original oval or circular frames are much sought after by collectors, especially when printed in sepia or colour (see also p53). Stipple engravings waned in popularity towards the middle of the 19th century when they were superseded by the development of lithography (see pp38–9).

Although stipple engraving was mainly confined to England, it probably developed from a French method of printing known as crayon manner engraving. This technique was used to reproduce the chalk drawings of artists such as Fragonard and Boucher and was popular until the French Revolution, when the fashion waned. The method involved drawing the design onto an etching ground using a special tool with a spiked wheel, known as a mattoir or roulette. These pitted the waxed surface exposing the copper beneath, which was then bitten with acid. The resulting prints differ from stipple engravings in that they are still essentially linear rather than tonal. Crayon manner engravings were usually printed in black and white or sepia red to simulate the effect of a red chalk drawing, sometimes on blue, grey or buff paper.

▲ **After Gaspard Poussin**
Arcadian Landscape, an etching by F.
Vivares published 1741 by C. Knapton.
The etching is on laid paper and in a
traditional "Hogarth" frame. **£80–120**

Etching

Etchings overcame the stiff appearance of
engraving by allowing the artist greater spontaneity and freedom in the creation of his image.
The plate was coated with an acid-resistant layer,
known as a "ground" – usually a mixture of wax and
bitumen. This was left to harden and the artist then
scratched his design into the black surface of the
ground using an etching needle, hence exposing the
metal beneath. The plate was then immersed in a
bath of dilute acid which bit into the metal in the
exposed areas only – so creating the incised image.
Tone could be varied by "stopping out" some
exposed areas, such as the background, which
would be covered with the ground after the initial
immersion, and the plate would be reimmersed in
the acid bath to create deeper incisions in other parts
of the design. The plate was then cleaned of the
ground and printing took place in the same way as
for an engraving (see pp24). Etchings had a far more
sketchy appearance than engravings, and are easily
confused with pen and ink drawings.

The earliest etchings date from the 16th century
and the technique has remained one of the most
popular printing methods to the present day. The
idea of producing an incised plate using acid probably developed from techniques used by metal
workers to decorate armour. The earliest etchings
were made on plates coated in a hard ground and
closely resemble the stiffness of engravings. Among
the most important early etchers were Lucas van
Leyden, Albrecht Altdorfer and Parmigianino.
Jacques Callot, another leading exponent, was an
engraver from Nancy who worked in Rome and
Florence and on his return in 1621 made a series of
bizarre and fantastic subjects including grotesque
beggars and subjects from the *Commedia dell'Arte*.
Callot's work was especially keenly collected during
the 18th century.

During the 17th century artists began experimenting with etchings made using a softer ground
which allowed the artist to draw as freely as he
would on paper. This allowed the artist to carry
small prepared plates with him and sketch directly
on to them, in much the same way as a note book
or sketch book. Etchings produced on this softer
ground (not to be confused with soft ground
etching, which is a separate technique) can be
distinguished from engravings by their sketchy

Veduta del Tempio di Giove Tonante

appearance – rather like a pen and ink drawing – and by the fact that the line on close examination is usually the same width, because it has been bitten by acid rather than created by pressure from the artist's burin and finishes in a blunt end rather than a tapering point. The first etcher to develop this new technique fully was Rembrandt who produced some 300 etched images drawn with incredible freedom and intensity (see p31).

During the 18th century etching was memorably used for large-scale architectural subjects, often in combination with engraving, by G. B. Piranesi (see also p56) and Rossini. In Spain Goya was one of the few Spanish artists to experiment with printmaking; his often rather menacing satirical prints were largely influenced by the technique of Rembrandt but the grotesque, nightmarish subjects also echo those etched by Callot two centuries earlier. Goya often combined etching with aquatint; among his best-known series are *Los Caprichos* (a set of 82 plates issued in 1799) and *Los Desastres de la Guerra* (80 plates published c.1800–18).

In England etching enjoyed a heyday of interest during the 19th century when numerous leading artists used it as a medium for printmaking. David Wilkie, a prominent Scottish artist associated with genre subjects, made etchings of domestic interiors. Other leading British etchers include Thomas Creswick, Charles West Cope, Edward Calvert and Samuel Palmer, who produced small upright plates and larger landscapes of idyllic pastoral subjects bathed in mysterious shimmering light. As the 19th century progressed etching became a popular medium for amateurs and even Queen Victoria and Prince Albert, instructed by Landseer, tried their hand at the fashionable art.

The popularity of etching continued through the late 19th century and into the 20th century both in England and Europe. On the Continent many of the leading artists of the day experimented with various printmaking techniques including etching; among them were Renoir, Pissarro, Millet, Corot, Degas and the Cubists. In England James Abbott McNeill Whistler made a series of celebrated etchings of the Thames and Venice; Charles Tunnicliffe produced charming etchings of farmyard animals. Other leading etchers include Frank Brangwyn, Muirhead Bone and James McBey.

▲ Drypoint etching
This detail shows the burr around
lines depicting the hair, and the
sketchy, spontaneous effect
characteristic of this technique.

► **Cyril Power**
The Railway Station, a
drypoint signed, titled and
inscribed "no 9". The rich,
velvety blackness of this
image is a good sign of an
early impression. Power is
also well-known for his lino
cuts (see pp20–21).
£400–500

Drypoint & Soft Ground Etching

The most direct and spontaneous of intaglio printing methods, drypoint involved scratching the design of an image straight on to a copper plate using an engraving needle. As the tool cut into the surface of the plate a burr of excised metal was thrown up on each side of the line. When the plate was inked both the incised line and the burr absorbed ink. The resulting printed image was made up of rather scratchy but distinctively furry lines often with a white line in the centre – caused by the burr absorbing enough ink to look like a separate line when printed. The burr that provides drypoints with their distinctive appearance wears quickly and when worn away the plate looks harsh and dull in comparison with the rich effect created with an early impression.

Drypoint was originally used to add extra detail to engravings and etchings. The first major artist to

develop the technique fully was Rembrandt who used drypoint in combination with etching to create images of unrivalled richness and depth. During the late 19th and early 20th centuries the technique was popular with many leading painters such as Mary Cassatt, Picasso, Derain, Whistler and Kandinsky, as well as artist-printmakers such as Edmund Blampied, Cyril Power and William Lionel Wyllie.

Soft ground etching, another intaglio printing method, evolved in the late 18th century as a way of imitating the softness of crayon, chalk or pencil drawing. Prints were made by coating a copper plate with an acid-resistant layer of soft tallow or resin that did not harden. The plate was then covered with a thin sheet of paper and the artist drew the design on to the sheet using a drawing tool. When the paper was gently removed the ground adhered to it in areas where the lines were drawn

▲ After George Morland
Washing by the River, a coloured soft ground etching by T. Vivares, was published in 1801 by S. W. Fores, one of the leading print publishers of the day. **£15–30**

Collecting Rembrandt etchings & drypoints

▲ Christ Healing the Sick
This etching with drypoint, c.1649, is one of Rembrandt's most famous prints. It is known as the "100 Guilder Print", such was the demand for it. This is the second of three states and therefore highly desirable. **£8,000–12,000**

Rembrandt Harmensz. van Rijn was not only the greatest Dutch painter but also the most influential and prolific printmaker of the 17th century. He probably learnt etching in Amsterdam where he worked after leaving the University of Leiden.

Rembrandt's use of chiaroscuro marks a departure from the hitherto rather linear images produced by etching. His prints are also distinctive for their use of "surface tone", an effect created by leaving a film of ink on the surface of the plate when it was printed, instead of wiping it completely clean as was previously the norm. As his style evolved he developed more effective tonal contrasts, and drypoint became increasingly important in his prints, giving added depth and richness to the images.

Rembrandt produced a total of some 300 etchings. His prints encompass an enormous variety of subjects, including family portraits, self-portraits, landscapes and religious scenes. Sizes vary considerably; there are 19 large plates, some measuring around 22 x 18in/56 x 46cm) and many on a very small scale. These plates were often extensively reworked by the artist before their final printing, and as he altered the plate, prints were made to gauge their effect. These are known as "states". Plates were also published after his death, sometimes after reworking by other artists. Values therefore range from tens of thousands of pounds to modest sums for later reprints. Most auction catalogues refer to the several *catalogues raisonnés* of Rembrandt's printed works which list the various states.

and pressure was applied. The plate was then immersed in acid; the exposed areas only being bitten created the effect of a slightly granular line, like that found on a drawing. This technique was popular with English artists in the late 18th century, particularly for reproducing landscape sketches. Among its most outstanding exponents were Thomas Gainsborough (who often used the method in conjunction with aquatint), John Constable, Paul Sandby, John Sell Cotman and Thomas Girtin. George Morland also used soft ground etching for his sketchier genre scenes.

Modern printmakers have further developed the technique and paper is no longer always used. The artist often draws directly through the ground using a blunt wooden instrument, and other textured objects such as leaves and fabric can be pressed into the ground to create a decorative effect.

► **After William Redmore Bigg ARA**
The Soldier's Widow, one of a pair of mezzotints by Robert Dunkarton, part-printed in colour with hand finishing, published 1800 by W. R. Bigg. **£800–1,000** the pair

◄ **After Johan Zoffany RA**
Portrait of Queen Charlotte, wife of George III, a mezzotint by Robert Sayer showing the incredible details of costume which the best engravers managed to incorporate in their work. **£200–300**

Mezzotints

Mezzotints were invented in the mid-17th century but enjoyed a heyday of popularity during the 18th and 19th centuries when they were much used to reproduce the richness of oil paintings. The term "mezzotint" comes from the Italian word *mezzatinta*, meaning half-tint, and the method effectively reproduced areas of graduated tone.

The technique was extremely laborious and time-consuming and involved roughening the entire surface of the copper plate with a rocker; this raised a burr on the surface and provided areas of deepest shadow, and the design was created by progressively smoothing back the areas of lighter tone. Mid-tones were therefore created by slightly polishing the roughed areas, while areas of highlight were achieved by polishing the plate completely smooth. When the plate was inked and wiped clean the most ink was retained by the most heavily textured areas, which therefore printed black; the smoother areas held less ink and provided paler gradations of tone, while polished areas held no ink at all and therefore printed completely white.

Early mezzotints were made using copper plates and, in the same way as drypoints, which also depend on the metal burr to create their effect, the plates wore down quickly and were short-lived. The best mezzotints are early impressions characterized by their rich, inky blackness. Later impressions tend to look grey and washed-out by comparison and are far less desirable. Mezzotint was often combined with etching and engraving which were used to give extra details; these are known as mixed mezzotints. Most were printed in black although some were printed in sepia and others part-printed in colour.

In the 19th century the life of mezzotint plates was extended by using steel rather than copper; these have a finer but harsher appearance but were used by many leading artists. The mezzotint technique has always been used mainly as a way of reproducing oil paintings and died out in the late 19th century, when it was largely replaced by photogravures (see p42). Mezzotints were particularly popular in England, and for this reason in France the method which at first was termed *manière noire* was later called *la manière anglaise*.

In the late 17th and 18th centuries mezzotints were mainly used to reproduce portraits after all the

▼ After Joshua Reynolds PRA
Portrait of Mrs Edward Lascelles, mezzotint by James Watson, an interesting proof before letters. On the bottom band the greyish tinge is caused by the rocker extending beyond the image; this would have been polished clean on the final image. **£100–200**

◄ Carington Bowles pub.
An English Sloop Engaging a Dutch Man of War, a humorous mezzotint with hand colouring typical of Carington Bowles, published in 1781. **£150–250**

► After Joseph Wright of Derby
A Blacksmith's Shop, a mezzotint of 1771 by Richard Earlom, one of the most accomplished mezzotinters of the day, published by J. Boydell, a leading publisher. Earlom was particularly adept at reproducing dramatic depths of shadow. **£700–900**

leading portraitists of the day such as Van Dyck, Kneller, Lely, Reynolds, Gainsborough, Hoppner and Romney. Some of the mezzotinters managed to incorporate astonishing details into the costumes of the sitter. One of the earliest pioneers of the technique was Prince Rupert, nephew of Charles I, who is thought to have invented the rocking tool used to create the necessary texture on the plate. Among the most celebrated early mezzotinters were Isaac Beckett, Valentine Green, John Raphael Smith, William Faithorne the Younger, Richard Earlom and John Faber (Older and Younger).

In the 19th century mezzotint was used to dramatic effect to reproduce the sublime and dramatic landscapes of Turner, Constable and John Martin. Turner's first important publication was *Liber Studiorum*, a folio of 71 plates published in parts between 1807–19. Turner himself made the sepia drawings and etched the outlines onto each plate which was then worked on by several commercial engravers including Charles Turner, George Clint and Thomas Lupton. Turner's other printed works in mezzotint include *The Little Liber* (unpublished) and *River Scenery*, or *Rivers of England*.

Mezzotints after John Constable's landscapes were made by David Lucas. Some prints were produced singly, others as part of a series published with text by the artist explaining his approach to painting, entitled *Various Subjects of English Landscape Scenery* and *A New Series of Engravings of English Landscape*.

The artist John Martin also made dramatic use of the effects of light and shade permitted by mezzotint. Martin worked on many of the plates himself and between 1820 and 1840 his output of apocalyptic and visionary landscape subjects acquired a huge market, so much so that numerous pirated copies of his work were produced. Many of Martin's mezzotints were published by Septimus Prowett. Among his best-known are illustrations to John Milton's *Paradise Lost*.

In a lighter vein were the series of humorous coloured mezzotints produced by the publisher Carington Bowles in the mid-18th century. These are heavily coloured by hand in thick gaudy gouache. Although the paint is often cracked and peels off, the subjects are appealing and remain highly popular with collectors.

◀ **Definition**
This detail shows the granular effect that is desirable. On later impressions this becomes blurred and almost disappears.

▼ **Topography**
Aquatint was ideally suited to reproducing scenery. This view of Winchester College after T. Taylor was engraved by F. C. Lewis. **£300–400**

◀ **After John Frederick Herring**
Jerry, the Winner of the Great St Leger, Doncaster 1824, part-printed in colour by Thomas Sutherland. Herring's St Leger winners, painted 1815–43, were published as aquatints and sold singly and in sets. **£200–400**

Aquatints

A sophisticated method of printing that simulates the tonal effect of watercolour paintings, aquatint was extremely popular in the late 18th and early 19th centuries. The basic aquatint technique involved covering a copper plate with a powdered or granulated layer of an acid-resistant substance. The plate was heated, making the grains melt and merge into one another to create an irregular speckled effect, and then allowed to cool and harden before being bitten in acid. The printed effect that this method created is one of randomly shaped white flecks surrounded by a darker ground. Gradations of tone were built up by stopping out: covering areas which were to print paler, such as the background, with varnish, and reimmersing the plate in the acid bath. The areas which were left exposed were therefore bitten more deeply and printed darker than those covered with varnish. Tone and texture were also controlled by varying the texture of the powder or granules used. The coarser the grains, the larger the acid-resistant spots created when the plate was heated which would therefore print as larger white or pale flecks.

There were several popular variations on this basic technique. One method was to suspend the granules in a solution of alcohol. This was painted on to the plate and when the alcohol evaporated it left behind a crystalline residue of grains which could then be bitten in the same way. This method is called "spirit ground aquatint". Another variation, known as "sugar lift", involved dissolving sugar in a solution of water tinted with ink. The artist painted his design onto the copper plate using this mixture and then covered it with a layer of varnish. When the varnish was dry the plate was immersed in water; this caused the sugar to dissolve, lifting the varnish in areas where the design was painted, and the plate could then be exposed to acid and printed in the usual manner.

Aquatints were first invented in France c.1760 by Jean-Baptiste Le Prince but it was in England that the technique became most popular. One of the first artists to explore its potential fully was Paul Sandby (1725–1809), a watercolourist who pioneered the spirit ground technique in order to create prints of a series of watercolours of Welsh scenery. These were published in 1776 as *XII Views in Aquatinta taken on the Spot in South Wales* and *XII Views in North Wales*; *XII Views in Wales* was published 1777. Sandby also published views of Windsor and Eton, and a series of views of military encampments. Sandby's prints enjoyed great success and were much reprinted as the print-buying public became increasingly interested in landscape subjects. His success led to a flurry of other topographical artists using the same technique to reproduce English scenery. Other accomplished exponents of aquatint include James Malton, who produced a sought-after series of views

▲ **After F. MacKenzie**
View of St John's College from the Gardens, a coloured aquatint by R. Reeve from two volumes containing 96 plates published in 1815 by Rudolph Ackermann on wove Whatman paper. The fresh colours and original bindings in which these plates survive make them highly sought after. **£2,000–3,000**

Collecting
Rudolph Ackermann prints

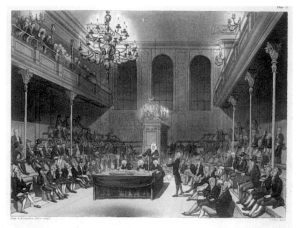

▲ **Rudolph Ackermann**
One of numerous aquatints of contemporary scenes published by Ackermann, this view of the House of Commons is by A. C. Pugin with figures by Thomas Rowlandson. **£30–50** upwards

of Dublin, and his nephew Thomas Malton who made a series of architectural aquatints of London. Aquatint was also popular for reproducing sporting subjects (see p65).

Early aquatints were printed in black and white and sometimes hand-coloured. Later some were part-printed in colour, and others printed in sanguine or sepia tone. Most artists, including Sandby, used aquatint in conjunction with etching to give the necessary detail and definition. Quality is judged on the crispness of the characteristic granular effect. Later impressions are identifiable by a blurring of the grains, often masked by coloured wash, and these are far less desirable.

One of the most famous European artists to experiment with the medium was Francisco de Goya who used aquatint, usually in conjunction with etching to give tone and depth to his printed images(see also p29). The technique has continued to be used this century by many prominent artists. Picasso used the method to illustrate *Histoire Naturelle* and *Poems of Gongora*.

Georges Rouault made numerous aquatints of circus subjects, and Tsuguharu Foujita, Georges Braque and Joan Miró also used the technique. In Britain, leading artist-printmakers who sometimes used aquatint, usually in conjunction with etching, included Henry Moore, John Piper and David Hockney.

Among the most interesting aquatints were scenes published by Rudolph Ackermann (1764–1834). His prints provide a fascinating record of contemporary English life in the late 18th and early 19th centuries. Ackermann published an illustrated magazine called *Repository of the Arts*, named after his shop, as well as single plates and books. His exhaustive range of subjects included topographical views of Oxford and Cambridge, contemporary interiors, decorative arts, botanical subjects and scenes of London life. Most earlier prints were in aquatint; later lithography was extensively used.

Prints were available by subscription or directly through his shop, which became a fashionable meeting place where customers were able to view prints without necessarily buying them. Ackermann commissioned works from many of the leading artists, designers and printmakers of the day. Most plates are marked with the artist's and engraver's name, although those from the *Repository of Arts* are often unsigned, and prices can vary according to the desirability of the subject. Topographical views, political subjects and good sporting prints are always highly sought after.

Planar Printing

From artists' lithographs to photomechanical printing processes

▲ James A. Grant
Maternity, a lithograph by Grant printed in colour in 1926. The registration cross outside the image used to align the colours is visible in the margin. Signed, dated and numbered 5/20 in pencil by the artist. **£30–40**

The 19th-century development of lithography is the most important final stage in the development of printing. All earlier printing methods, however diverse, had relied upon the difference in level between background and image to hold ink and thus print the design. Lithography differed dramatically in that the printmaker achieved his image from a completely flat surface; hence images created by printing methods of this type are generically known as "planar" or "lanographic" prints.

The word "lithography" is derived from the ancient Greek word "litho", meaning stone, and the first lithographs were literally stone drawings. The technique relied on the fact that greasy substances attract one another and that water and grease are incompatible. At its simplest the image was drawn onto a polished stone (originally a type of limestone from Bavaria that was porous and thus held water well), using a greasy crayon. The image was then chemically fixed and the stone dampened with water. The water was absorbed by the porous limestone except in the parts sealed by the crayon. When a greasy ink was then rolled over the surface of the stone the water absorbed by the stone repelled the ink, and was chemically attracted to the drawn design. The image was transferred to paper by placing a sheet of paper on the stone and passing them through a press (see p12).

Coloured or tinted lithographs were created using the same method, but usually with a different stone for each colour used and the various stones were lined up using a small cross with a hole, known as a registration mark. These marks can often be visible at the edge of the print. Stones were large and expensive and a surprising number of artists therefore reused stones by grinding down the surface and therefore eradicating the image once the edition was printed. Stones were superseded by zinc and aluminium plates towards the end of the 19th century. The versatility of the technique means that lithographs can vary widely in appearance. They can resemble pen and ink drawings,

◄ Charles Hazelwood Shannon *Reclining Nude*, an early 20th-century lithograph signed in pencil and published by W. Stacey. Shannon used lithography extensively, and this composition is typically soft and lively in appearance. The print has slight foxing, probably caused by the acidic mount which is discoloured and needs replacing. **£300–400**

chalk drawings or coloured wash drawings. There is no plate mark as you would find with an intaglio print, and the ink is not raised but lies flat on the surface of the paper; though very occasionally you can see where the stone or plate has flattened the surface of the paper when it was exposed to pressure in the press.

One disadvantage of early lithographs was that images drawn directly onto stone were reversed when printed. To avoid this the design was drawn onto transfer paper – which had first been treated with a soluble substance such as gelatin – using a greasy crayon. Once the design was complete the paper was dampened and then inverted onto the stone – as the ground dissolved the design came away from the paper and stuck to the stone. When the stone was printed in the normal way, the image was no longer reversed.

Lithography was invented in Germany in 1798 by Aloys Senefelder and as the 19th century progressed it was developed both by commercial printers, who realized that it could provide a highly economical method of mechanically reproducing coloured printed images, and by artists who enjoyed the diverse range of effects they could achieve. "Chromolithographs" or "chromos" are terms often used to describe the vast quantities of commercial mechanically produced colour lithographs produced in the late 19th century, as distinct from hand-coloured lithographs made by artists in limited quantity.

Offset lithography was another method which evolved to overcome the problem of printing a reversed image. This involves printing from the stone or metal plate onto a rubber-coated cylinder which is then printed onto paper. Offset techniques are sometimes used by artists to reproduce their work but, as with any collectable 20th-century print, examples should be signed and numbered by hand, by the artist. The offset technique is also used to reproduce images photographically. These images, known as "photo litho offset", are often identifiable by the tiny dots from which the image is composed and are rarely of interest to the collector.

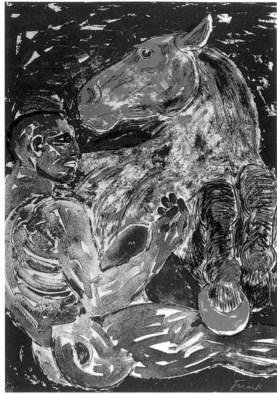

Lithographs

The technique of lithography allowed artists unprecedented freedom of expression, since they could draw directly onto the stone or transfer paper in the same way as they would make a drawing (see p12). Not surprisingly the method was quickly adopted by many leading artists. In France one of the most prolific early exponents was the artist and satirist Honoré Daumier, who produced over 4,000 lithographs.

Senefelder, the inventor of lithography, introduced the technique to England in 1800, when he sold patents to publishers J. & P. Andre. Among the first English artists to begin using the method were the President of the Royal Academy, Benjamin West, and Fuseli. Other early publishers of lithographs include Rudolph Ackermann who used the method to reproduce prints for his *Repository of Arts* and other publications.

From the 1820s onwards as lithography evolved, the technique was much used to reproduce topographical illustrations both in England and in France. David Roberts' drawings made on his travels in Spain, Morocco, Egypt and Palestine were printed in this way by Louis Haghe. Roberts' work was popular and many later versions were published, both in England, Europe and America, some with illustrations reduced photographically. In France vast numbers of topographical subjects were lithographically reproduced for Baron Taylor's publication *Voyages Pittoresques et Romantiques dans l'Ancienne France*. Other topographical artists whose work was much reproduced as lithographs at this time were Samuel Prout, Richard Parkes Bonington and Edward Lear.

Among the leading artists who used lithography in the late 19th century was Degas, who found the technique ideally suited to reproducing chalk drawings, and Pierre Bonnard who introduced the technique to Toulouse-Lautrec. One of the major influences on the appearance of lithographs at this time was the interest in Japanese woodcuts, which were just reaching the West. Lautrec's prolific lithographs – he made 370 – have long been highly sought after and all are well documented and

Pastoral scene, one of a set of 16 sporting and pastoral lithographs published in 1826, showing how lithography could be used to reproduce the effect of a pencil drawing. The foxing is caused by impurities in the paper – often seen on 19th-century lithographs. **£400–500** (for 16 prints)

◀ **After David Roberts**
Fountain of Job, Valley of Hinnom, a coloured lithograph. One of a set of five, published 1842–9 in *The Holy Land, Syria, Idumea, Arabia, Egypt and Nubia*. From the first edition by F. G. Moon. **£1,200–1,800** (for the set)

exhaustively catalogued. Most have been widely reprinted and reproduced however, and collectors should only buy from reputable sources.

In the 19th century the evolution of colour lithography became increasingly mechanized, as did the production of paper where chemicals were added to break down the fibres. Over the passage of time these impurities can react with atmospheric conditions and cause foxing (see p148), a problem often encountered with Roberts' lithographs.

Most artists at this time were content to let their work be transferred to stone and be published in lithographic form by professionals. Leading names include Charles Hullmandel – who worked both as lithographer and publisher and pioneered the development of tinted lithographs – and the publishers Day & Sons.

In the 20th century the lithographic process has continued to attract the attentions of many artists. James Abott McNeill Whistler, who is also known for his etchings, produced humorous lithographs too, and his work was influential on the work of English artists such as William Rothenstein and Charles Hazelwood Shannon, who excelled in creating delicately drawn images that look as if they are done in lead pencil. Whistler was also largely responsible for introducing the use of a pencil signature to artist's prints to control their production, charging double the amount for a signed print. The pencil signature has now become a virtual prerequisite of most artist's prints. Later in the century artists such as Elisabeth Frink, Henry Moore, John Piper and Howard Hodgkin have continued to use the technique, while on the Continent many of the leading artists of the School of Paris produced lithographs in prolific quantities (see pp86–7).

Prices for lithographs vary enormously depending on the status of the artist and the rarity and appeal of the subject matter. Topographical subjects by lesser artists, French satirical prints and illustrations from 19th-century magazines are often sold unframed in multi-lots at auction for modest prices, but, in contrast, early lithographs by David Roberts are increasingly sought after and valuable.

▲ Sporting subjects
Chromolithographs such as this example were published in magazines and are available for modest sums. £10–15

▼ Royal portraits
Chromolithographs provided an inexpensive alternative to an original work of art, and royal subjects such as this portrait of Queen Victoria were especially popular. The acidic backboard has caused discoloration on the image, which will reduce its value considerably. £20–50

Chromolithographs & Oleographs

The term "chromolithograph" is nowadays usually used to differentiate between the mass-produced colour lithographs produced by highly commercial printing methods mainly in the second half of the 19th century, and hand-made artists' lithographs which were generally made in limited numbers and remain far more valuable to collectors today.

Until the late 19th century the term "chromolithography" was used to describe any colour-printed lithographic image. The technique developed in the 19th century in England and France as a way of reproducing colour images. The method was first patented in 1837 by Godefroy Engelmann, a Paris-based lithographer who developed a method of using three primary colours, each printed separately, to create an entirely mechani-cally printed colour image. Before this, tinted litho-graphs had been produced using a second stone and extra colour was added by hand. Similar colour printing processes also evolved in England soon afterwards, and one of the pioneers of colour lithog-raphy was the lithographer Charles Hullmandel.

As specially manufactured inks became available and other technical problems were overcome in the second half of the 19th century, chromolith-ography became less expensive and quantities of colour-printed images were produced. Many chro-molithographs use a wide range of colours and at least two shades of each colour to provide light and dark areas. Some mid-19th-century printmakers used stippled colours to create a subtler effect; others relied on flat areas of colour which tend to be garish with a rather lifeless appearance to the surface.

Illustration from *Fleurs, Fruits et Feuillage* by P. Depannemaker, typical of the late 19th-century botanical chromolithographs that are colourful but still affordable. **£50–100**

▲ **Birds and animals**
English chromolithograph of a red-winged starling, 19th century. Prints of this type were often originally made for book illustrations. **£10–15**

Chromolithography was a popular method of illustrating books and many of the wildlife, botanical and fashion plates sold in print galleries today for modest sums started life as book illustrations made using this method of printing. Chromolithography was also used to reproduce old master paintings, particularly of religious subject matter.

The oleograph was a popular variation of the chromolithograph that also proliferated during the late 19th century. Oleographs employ the same basic method of printing but an oily ink was used and the image was reproduced onto a textured surface – either cloth or board – that was then heavily varnished and framed in the manner of an oil painting. The finished effect was intended to simulate oil paintings often with great success and even today novice collectors are often confused into thinking that oleographs after works by well-known masters are genuine oil paintings, especially when the "canvas" is seen from the reverse.

Both chromolithographs and oleographs are among the least expensive types of print to buy, and their collectability depends chiefly on the decorative appeal of their subject. Large colourful prints of birds or similarly popular subjects may attract surprisingly high prices, especially if they are attractively framed and mounted, but religious subjects and prints after old masters are far less appealing to modern tastes and as such have little value as collectables.

Chromolithographs were often printed on inexpensive wood pulp paper, and over time exposure to atmospheric acidity can cause foxing. Condition is therefore an important consideration since less valuable prints are rarely worth expensive restorations.

Other Printing Methods

Photomechanical methods, Baxter prints, screen prints and monotypes

▲ **Grace Darling**
Unsigned Baxter print depicting the Victorian heroine Grace Darling. In 1838, the daughter of a lighthouse keeper on the Farne Islands saved nine marooned sailors by rowing through a storm to their sinking ship. **£15–20**

Throughout the 19th century industrial progress and economic prosperity fuelled a continuing demand for more effective economical printing, giving rise to numerous variations in the techniques already developed. The greatest new development came in the mid-19th century with the development of photomechanical printmaking techniques. These were made possible by the development of light-sensitive chemicals that were acid-resistant.

Among a wide variety of photographic techniques that emerged over the following decades were line block printing and half-tone block printing – both photographic developments of relief printing; photogravure and rotogravure – photographic relief methods; and photolithography and collotypes – both planar methods. Many of these methods remained popular well into the 20th century and they are all known by the generic term of "photomechanical printing methods".

Photomechanical prints fall largely outside the scope of this book since they were rarely used by artist-printmakers and, unless their subject matter makes them particularly interesting, are seldom of interest to collectors. Nevertheless, the techniques are noteworthy because they revolutionized the appearance of illustrated books and magazines.

Another successful 19th-century method of printing was patented by George Baxter in the 1830s. His products were instantly popular and are still highly sought after by collectors today. Baxter's method created high-quality colour prints and involved combining relief and intaglio methods. The image was first made on a metal plate using a technique such as aquatint, and then coloured using the relief wood block method. Baxter's prints are remarkable for the great number of different colours used, each of which required a different block to print from, sometimes up to 20 separate blocks were used to create a single coloured image.

▶ Terry Frost
*Oh what an effort it is
to love you as I do...*
Silkscreen printed in
colours, signed and
numbered by the artist
in pencil. The print was
contained in a portfolio of
48 lithographs, etchings,
lino cuts and silkscreens
published by the Royal
College of Art in celebration
of the college's 150th
anniversary and contained
work by many leading
20th-century artists.
£1,200–1,500 for the
portfolio (**£50–100**
individually)

The narrow dividing line between reproductive photographic processes and hand-made "original" processes became ever more blurred thanks to a popular new form of printing that emerged in the 20th century. Screen prints, also known as silkscreen or serigraphy, were made using a taut gauze sheet attached to a rigid frame; the design was created by stopping out areas of the mesh, using a stencil or various other methods (see pp13 and 46). During the 1960s the technique was further developed so that photographic images could be turned into stencils and embedded in the mesh to print in the same way. This type of photographic screenprint is particularly associated with pop artists and most memorably with Andy Warhol and Roy Lichtenstein. Despite the technique's reliance on photography, these are nevertheless generally accepted as "artist's prints" and as such are keenly collected.

Monotype is another printing method that has become increasingly popular with artists of the 20th century. In contrast to many of the more sophisticated developments of recent decades, monotypes are perhaps the most elemental of all printing types. The word "monotype" means single image, and as the name suggests, these are usually "one off" prints, made by painting the image directly onto a sheet of glass, metal or plastic, placing a sheet of paper over it and applying pressure by hand or with a press. Although the method only yields one strong impression, second and third images can sometimes be printed from the same plate. This method is much used nowadays in combination with etching, which is used to provide an outline for the image that is then printed in colour. The advantage of the method lies in the fact that every print will look different, and the colours can be mixed together with great freedom. The disadvantages are that monotypes are extremely time-consuming for the artist to produce, and thus print runs are usually limited to very small numbers.

◀ **Genre subjects**
This typically sentimental Victorian print entitled *So Nice*, 1852, was originally published with a companion piece entitled *I Don't Like it...* The plate was also used by Le Blond.
£15–20

Baxter Prints

Baxter prints were the first widely available type of colour print. Made by an innovatory colour printing process developed by George Baxter in the mid-19th century, they enjoyed phenomenal success and were sold in their millions. Today, although still popular with collectors, Baxters are available for very modest sums. Subjects include religious scenes, military subjects, landscapes, topography, political events and sentimental scenes, all of which combined to provide a fascinating visual record of the fashions and events that took place during the Victorian age.

Baxter started his working career as a printer in his father's business in Sussex, and in 1829, after settling in London, began producing his first colour prints. His printing method involved creating an image from an intaglio metal plate, usually a mixture of aquatint and etching, which was then coloured with wood blocks inked in oil colours. An unprecedented number of colours were applied, each using separate blocks. At least 10 colours were used for each image but on the most elaborate up to 30 different colours were separately applied. The overall effect of richly varied colour combined with softness from the use of aquatint appealed greatly to the Victorian love of decorative and elaborately detailed images.

Baxter patented his process in 1835 and prints were made both as book illustrations and to be sold as individual prints, the latter often ready-mounted on embossed card. His early work was published by the London Missionary Society and includes religious subjects and large prints of Queen Victoria's coronation. After 1845 Baxter began making smaller less expensive prints to decorate the lids of needle boxes. Measuring 6 x 5in/15 x 13cm each, needle box prints were produced in series of 10 or 12 which could be collected by the keen needlewomen of the day. One of the most popular sets was the *Regal* series, featuring scenes from Victoria's

◀ ▲ *Her Most Gracious Majesty the Queen*,
and *His Royal Highness Prince Albert*
These are among the most popular of Baxter prints,
dating from 1850, and were the first to be signed
by him in the image. Smaller versions of the same
subject were printed as part of the *Regal* series and
the plates were reprinted by Le Blond. **£30–40**

coronation and the marriage of the Queen and
Prince Consort; other series included fairy scenes
and prints after famous religious paintings. Before
Baxter's patent finally expired in 1854 he licensed
his printing method to several other printers including Le Blond, Bradshaw & Blacklock, Joseph
Martin Knonheim, William Dickes, Joseph Mansell
and Myers & Co., and several other non-licensed
printers also adopted the Baxter method.

The most popular subjects, such as Jenny Lind
(the Swedish Nightingale), were published in huge
numbers – over 300,000 in certain cases, and millions of smaller album illustrations were sold. When
Baxter sold his business to Le Blond, the most
famous of his licensees, in 1860, Le Blond continued
to print from some of Baxter's most popular plates.
Le Blond gave serial numbers and titles to all his
prints and produced a series of oval prints which
were printed onto mounts with embossed rims with
the title and period number embossed on a panel.

All prints made using the Baxter method, even
those made by licensees, are known as "Baxter
prints" and they are usually easily identifiable by the
fact that the name of the licensee is usually displayed
in the mount. The prints are usually small-scale and
if closely examined the image will be seen to be
made up from a granular base, sometimes printed in
brown, filled with clearly defined blocks of colour.

Although Baxters once enjoyed great popularity
as a collecting area, their value has fallen in recent
years, and for collectors on a budget this is a field
with huge potential. Value depends on size, subject
and condition; the most desirable prints are those of
royalty and the series *Gems of the Great Exhibition*.
Other subjects, unless rare, are worth small sums.
Examples by Baxter or Le Blond tend to be of better
quality and are more sought after than those by
other licensees. Baxter prints are vulnerable to damage and it is worth looking for those with their
original mount and title or serial number intact.

▼ **Paul Gaugin**
Paysage des Marquises avec un personnage, or *Le Paradis*
Gouache monotype printed in burgundy, two shades of blue, orange, green, purple and white, c.1902, on buff imitation japan. In good condition with slight discoloration, this was valued at **£100,000–120,000**.

Screen Printing & Monotypes

Screen printing differs from the main printing methods in that it is an indirect method of printing. Instead of creating an image by pressing one surface to which ink has been applied onto another, screen printing is achieved by using a third element – the screen through which the ink must pass to create the image.

The technique varies but, at its simplest, involves making a stencil of the areas not to be printed using film, paper or card and placing this under a mesh-covered frame. The mesh usually consists of woven silk – hence the term silkscreen by which this method is also known – but metal, synthetic fabrics or cotton are also sometimes used. Ink poured at the bottom of the screen is spread evenly across its surface using a "squeegee", a flexible rubber blade. Pressure from the squeegee forces the ink through the mesh only in areas not stopped out by the stencil and onto the paper below. Different stencils can be used to build up colour and pattern and the screen is either washed between printing each colour, or more commonly different screens are used (see p13).

Screen printing is among the least expensive of printing methods; it in fact emerged in the United States in the 1930s during the Depression when it enabled artists to create colourful printed images at very little expense. The method is also very much linked to textile printing and has remained popular in art schools and colleges. In recent decades screen-printing has been used by many leading contemporary artists such as Peter Blake, Elisabeth Frink, Claes Oldenburg and Victor Pasmore.

The basic technique has been further developed by dispensing with the stencil and painting the design directly onto the screen using a "liquid stencil" or screen filler. The filler has to be resistant to the solvent in the ink, so that the stencil does not dissolve during the printing process or when the screen is washed. This method allows the artist far more freedom to create spontaneous painterly images which look as if they have been "drawn" rather than "cut" from a stencil.

Both stencil and filler screen prints create prints which are the "negative" of the image the artist has drawn. Another development of screen printing, the "tusche" method, overcame this problem by creating "positive" images. Tusche is a type of black ink made from the greasy constituents used in lithographic crayons. Using this liquid the artist paints his design directly onto the screen. The entire surface of the screen is then coated in water-soluble

3/48   *Irvin '87*

◄ **Patrick Caulfield**
Fruit Bowl, published by
Waddington and numbered
80/100. Colours on screen prints
are typically more thickly applied
than on lithographs. **£200–300**

▲ **Albert Irvin**
A screenprint produced
in colours, entitled *Galaxy*,
signed and dated '87 and
numbered in pencil.
£50–100

glue which is allowed to set and harden. The glue does not stick to the tusche and when the screen is rinsed in spirit, the tusche dissolves, leaving the mesh exposed where the design was painted, but the glue "background" intact. The printed image is therefore the same as the one painted by the artist. Other important developments in screen printing include the transfer of photographic images into stencils using light-sensitive materials (see also p43).

Screen prints are most easily confused with lithography but can usually be identified by the thickness of the ink which lies on the surface of the paper and often looks flat, and by the texture of the mesh which is sometimes visible in the surface of the ink. As with any modern artist's print, screen prints are usually signed in pencil and numbered.

Monotype printing is believed to have been invented by Giovanni Battista Castiglione but the method remained little used throughout the 17th, 18th and early 19th centuries. Among the handful of artists who tried their hand at monoprinting around the turn of the 19th century were George Chinnery and William Blake. One of the most famous artists to experiment with monotype in the 19th century was Edgar Degas, who is believed to have made around 400 impressions using this technique. Degas

not only used the usual method of painting the design directly onto a plate – known as the "light field manner" – but also tried his hand at the "dark field manner", a method in which the plate was covered with ink and the composition formed by drawing into its inked surface – creating white lines on a dark ground. Other well-known contemporaries of Degas who used the same technique include Mary Cassatt, Camille Pissarro, Paul Gauguin and Toulouse-Lautrec.

The monotype enjoyed a peak of popularity with British artists in the 1930s and 1940s when among the leading printmakers to use the method were Cyril Power and Sybil Andrews (better known for their lino cuts), and the Polish artist Jankel Adler who introduced the method to many contemporary artists. The method has remained popular with printmakers today and variations include creating linear drawings by covering the plate with ink, laying a sheet of paper over, and drawing the image on the back of the paper using the wooden end of a paintbrush or a similar hard blunt instrument. When the paper is lifted the impression looks "drawn" but softened by the smudges of ink that transfer to the paper by inadvertent pressure from the artist's hand during the printing process.

Narrative Prints

Decorative and domestic scenes, caricatures, satire and humour

During the 17th century prints after genre paintings and famous works of art found a growing audience and were an important method of spreading new artistic ideas throughout Europe. As prints became increasingly widely available and printmaking became accepted as a medium in its own right, decorative subjects depicting pastoral scenes, family life, young lovers and mythological subjects provided an affordable alternative to oils and watercolours. Such subjects enjoyed a heyday of popularity in the late 18th century and early 19th century and continued to be produced until the early years of the 20th century.

In England one of the pioneers of both the narrative scene and the satirical print was Hogarth, who made series of engravings after his paintings which related a moral tale and satirized contemporary society (see p25).

Towards the end of the 18th century, interest in subjects with a moral theme, or of purely decorative content, was boosted by the development of new printing techniques, such as stipple engraving, which made possible the increasingly subtle depiction of such pictorial subject matter. Most narrative scenes were adapted from paintings. Some subjects were printed in sepia, simulating sanguine chalk drawings, as an alternative to the more common black ink, and many of the best-quality prints were part-printed in colour and finished with hand colouring. Unlike botanical or architectural prints genre subjects were never intended to be part of a connoisseur's portfolio. Reflecting the prevailing tastes in interior design, they would have been hung on the wall; today they are often found in their original *verre eglomise* mounts and elaborate gilded frames.

For many years genre prints were largely ignored by serious collectors, but recently they have attracted the attentions of interior designers and prices have risen dramatically, especially for those in original frames or of circular or oval form. Many of the best-loved genre subjects remained popular long after they were first printed and numerous later editions were made. Collectors of such well-known subjects should look for good clear impressions and early paper. The 19th-century vogue for pasting prints into scrap books means that decorative prints can often be found in albums, frequently at a fraction of the cost of framed examples, if you are willing to hunt through such volumes at auction.

◄ **After George Morland**
Idleness, one of a pair of oval stipple engravings by C. Knight part-printed in colour, showing the typically decorative subject matter, often with a moral overtone, that proliferated at the end of the 18th and early 19th centuries. £500–700

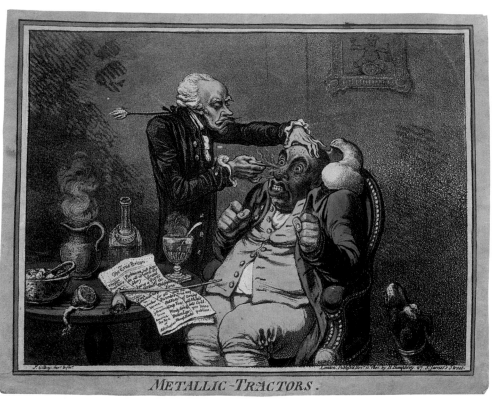

► **James Gillray**
Metallic Tractors, a coloured etching with aquatint published by H. Humphrey in 1801. The gruesome subject and bright, gaudy colouring are typical of satirical prints of the period. £100–200

METALLIC-TRACTORS.

The obvious decorative appeal of narrative and genre scenes is in stark contrast to the plethora of satirical cartoons that were produced from the 18th century onwards. Caricature drawings were made by artists in Italy and northern Europe from the Renaissance period although their potential as a subject for printmakers was not fully explored until the 18th century, when they were widely used as a way to criticize social and political excess.

Throughout the 18th and early 19th centuries satirical prints were increasingly produced both by amateur and professional printmakers who used them as a medium to denounce and poke fun at unpopular political policies, royal excesses and social pretension in general. Today, although their subject matter is often extremely obscure to all but the most specialist historians, their robust drawing and crude colouring have great charm and they provide a fascinating alternative insight into the society of the day.

During the 18th and early 19th centuries, satirical subject matter of the type published by James Gillray, Thomas Rowlandson, George Cruickshank and their contemporaries was generally termed "caricature". The word "cartoon" referred to a preparatory drawing for a work of art until the 19th century, when designs entered for frescoes to decorate the House of Commons were mocked in the magazine *Punch* and the word became associated with humorous drawings or prints.

The value of caricatures is largely dependent on subject matter. Scenes featuring doctors, lawyers and dentists are especially popular with modern-day collectors of the same profession and often command a premium. Royal subjects are also enduringly popular, and several well-known politicians are avid collectors of political cartoons. Later reprints are widely available at a fraction of the cost of good early impressions. Many of Gillray's most famous prints, reprinted in book form in monochrome in the late 19th century, have been taken apart and coloured at a later date. Identifiable by their washy colours and later paper, these versions are far less desirable than the rather gaudy, hand-coloured originals. Although in the 20th century cartoons and caricatures remain popular, for the most part original drawings and artworks are relatively affordable and few limited edition prints are made.

► **Thomas Rowlandson**
Dr Syntax made free of the Cellar,
a coloured aquatint from the famous
Dr Syntax series published by R.
Ackermann in 1820. **£20–40**

▲ **After James Gillray**
Paving the way for a Royal Divorce,
a coloured etching by C. Williams
published in 1816 by Johnston.
Though made after Gillray's
retirement, the print's royal subject
matter boosts its value. **£50–80**

► ***The Four Greens!!!***
A hand-coloured
engraving satirizing
fashionable dress by the
caricaturist T. Jones,
published by S. W. Fores
in 1827. **£100–200**

Cartoons, Caricatures & Satirical Prints

The term "caricature" comes from the Italian word "caricare", meaning to load, and caricatures were initially exaggerated portrait drawings. Leonardo da Vinci made such studies of grotesque faces in the 15th century and by the 16th century caricature drawing, in which mockery and fun were an intrinsic part of the overall effect, was being produced by many leading Italian artists. By the late 17th century caricatures in the form of prints began to become popular and Italian artists such P. L. Ghezzi began to direct their attentions towards the affluent English aristocrats who congregated in Rome on their Grand Tour. Thomas Patch, an English artist-engraver working in Italy, also produced tongue-in-cheek caricatures of English tourists in Rome and Florence, many of which were inoffensive enough to be bought by those they portrayed.

Satirical prints also gave printmakers a golden opportunity to comment on political events. In France in the 17th century, prints criticizing the policies of Louis XIV were made, usually by Dutch engravers. Roman de Hooge reflected Dutch disapproval of the French invasion of Holland with a memorable print showing Louis sitting on top of the world in the process of receiving an enema. Political

prints took a little longer to catch on in England, but by the mid-18th century George Marquess of Townshend became one of the pioneers of the British satirical print when he published caricatures of politicians. Matthew Darly, a printmaker and retailer, was also quick to appreciate the demand for such subject matter and in 1756 began to publish a series entitled *A Political and Satyrical History*.

By the turn of the 19th century the freedom of the press enabled English printmakers to produce topical satirical prints that attempted to influence public opinion on royal policies and political events of the day. By far the two most famous artists of such subjects were Thomas Rowlandson and James Gillray.

Rowlandson studied in Paris and at the Royal Academy and began producing his humorous subjects around 1780. Among Rowlandson's most famous subjects are his series entitled *The Miseries of Life* (1808) and *The Tours of Dr Syntax* (1812–20), both published by Ackermann. Rowlandson's subjects are notable for their humanity and compassion, even when portraying scenes of low life.

In contrast, his most famous contemporary, James Gillray, concentrated on attacking the follies of George III and his son George IV, in a far more

◀ **Louis Léopold Boilly**
La Félicité parfaite (one of a pair produced with *Les Cancans*); a coloured lithograph published by Delpech. **£200–300** for the pair

▼ **James Gillray**
The Nutcracker, a German Toy; coloured etching published 1816 by Johnston. Not uncommonly, this has been pasted on a backing sheet and has residual staining at the corners that reduces value. **£40–60**

◀ **After Thomas Rowlandson**
Amputation, a gruesome etching with aquatint, published by S. W. Fores. A particularly early impression sold for **£1,800** as part of a pair.

crude and vitriolic way. Gillray achieved his early success in the field of satirical printmaking with *A New Way to Pay the National Debt* (pub. 1786), in which he poked fun at the royal family. Hugely popular in his own lifetime, Gillray's work over the next two decades (he ceased work due to bouts of insanity c.1810) reflected his often scurrilous opinions and mirrored all the major events of the day, from the marriage of Princess Charlotte to the enormously plump Duke of Württemberg, to the Napoleonic wars, and, most memorably, the worst excesses of the Prince Regent, later George IV.

Two of his most memorable royal portraits are *Temperance Enjoying a Frugal Meal*, a caricature of George III poking fun at his meanness, and its pendant *A Voluptuary Under the Horrors of Digestion*, a critique of his son's extravagance. One of the most popular Napoleonic images is entitled *The King of Brobdingnag and Gulliver* (1804), and shows Napoleon as a Lilliputian rowing a model boat on the bath with George III and Queen Charlotte looking on. Many of Gillray's prints originally published by H. Humphrey and S. W. Fores have been reprinted by Johnston and others. Thin bright hand colouring is typical of early prints. Reprints of his

work have often been coloured at a later date and look washy by comparison with original colouring.

George Cruickshank quickly established himself as a popular successor to Gillray. His caricatures detail the worst excesses of Regency fashion including a famous series entitled *Monstrosities*. Later works reflect the moralizing preoccupation of the Victorian age, often relating to the dangers of alcohol abuse; his most famous is a series of six woodcuts called *The Bottle* (pub. 1847). Other leading English caricaturists of the late 18th and 19th centuries include Robert Dighton, William Henry Bunbury, Thomas Jones, William Dent, Richard Newton, William Heath and John Doyle, who used the monogram HB.

In France artists had less freedom to express themselves in such a way. Despite this atmosphere of censorship, one of the most important caricaturists of the 19th century was Honoré Daumier, who produced political lithographs that were published in Charles Philipon's controversial publication *Caricature*. The French establishment was, however, less tolerant of such critiques, and Daumier was imprisoned for his attacks on the restored monarch Louis-Philippe.

▶ **19th-century French School**

Me soupçonner, moi!!! On ne passe pas sans payer, a coloured lithograph by de Villain. Published by the leading French publisher Martinet.
£100–200

▼ **After Jean-Baptiste Huet**

La Souper, a well-defined, mixed method engraving, one from a set of three. On later impressions the image looks flatter and muddy.
£200–300 for the set

◀ **After George Morland**

The Fruits of Oeconomy and Early Industry (shown here) and *The Effects of Extravagance*, one of a pair of stipple engravings by J. L. Darcis, published 1800. The white paper is misleading and in this case does not indicate a reprint but overcleaning.
£200–300 the pair.

Decorative Genre Subjects

The term "genre" prints may sound rather academic and daunting, but the word is simply the French word meaning "type", and has come to mean prints (or paintings) featuring people in scenes from everyday life. Genre subjects first became popular in the Low Countries in the 17th century, when artists such as Breughel, Teniers and van Ostade painted scenes of peasants working and carousing. These scenes were disseminated as engravings and etchings throughout Europe, and the tradition was developed in England with Hogarth's scenes of London life.

During the late 18th and 19th centuries, increasing numbers of newly affluent picture-buyers wanted affordable decorative images, and attractive scenes, often with a moral undertone, enjoyed a peak of popularity which lasted until the early years of the 20th century. Nostalgic scenes of rustic simplicity, courting couples, the contrast between youth and age, industry and idleness, classical maidens and beautiful lovelorn ladies in compromising situations were staple subjects for painters and printmakers who capitalized on the demand for this type of sentimental print.

Decorative genre subjects remain extremely popular with modern-day collectors and price is dramatically affected by the appeal of the image. The present market especially favours attractive children, cherubs and classical subjects. Prints in sepia or colour are far more desirable than those in black and white. Prices can also be dramatically increased if a print is one of a pair or a set or in an original frame. Many prints framed in the 18th and 19th centuries had their margins heavily trimmed and the print line was often cut off and pasted onto the back board. If this has remained on the frame it can provide valuable information as to the date and origin of the print and is always worth preserving, even if the print needs remounting or new backing.

Among the best-known artists of popular decorative and genre subjects in the 19th century were Angelica Kauffmann, Giovanni Battista Cipriani, Richard Westall, Henry Singleton, Charles Ansell, Francis Wheatley, Adam Buck, William Hamilton

◀ **After William Redmore Bigg**
Saturday Evening: The Husband's Return from Labour, stipple engraving part-printed in colour by W. Nutter. One of a pair (see p23). For the pair: **£300–500**

▶ **After François-Louis Soinard**
La Toilette de la Mariée, stipple engraving by Paul Tassaert, published in Paris. Inexpensive decorative genre prints such as these are often found pasted into scrapbooks and albums. **£20–30**

▲ **Circular and oval prints**
Framed circular and oval prints, such as this after Sir Joshua Reynolds by Francesco Bartolozzi, the most famous stipple engraver, are always especially desirable if part-printed in colour. **£150–250**

and George Morland. The refined tonal techniques perfected in the 18th century were ideally suited to genre subjects; some were mezzotints printed in colour; others were printed using stipple engraving and aquatint, and in the 19th century lithography was used. The most expensive prints were those part-printed in colour and hand-finished, and these command a premium today. Less expensive monochrome editions of the most popular series would also have been available; these have sometimes been coloured by hand at a later date. Throughout the centuries prints of inexpensive monochrome genre subjects were often collected and pasted into albums, and these are often available in print sales for relatively modest sums.

Well-known engravers of genre subjects include Francesco Bartolozzi (see p26), who had trained with Cipriani in Rome, and who trained numerous pupils himself. Bartolozzi produced a huge variety of stipple engravings after the classical subjects of Angelica Kauffmann, and his work is always sought after by collectors. Other engravers include J. Louis

Darcis, a French stipple engraver, who made plates after George Morland and Henry Singleton, such as *The Fruits of Oeconomy and Early Industry.* Most of these subjects were made after paintings, sometimes specially commissioned by publishers who were keen to exploit the demand for such material. One of the most famous genre series ever produced was the *Cries of London,* a series of 13 stipple engravings, commissioned and first published by Colnaghi, Sala & Co in 1793–7, after paintings by Francis Wheatley. The stipple engravers involved included Bartolozzi, his pupil Luigi Schiavonetti, Antoine Cardon and Giovanni Vendramini .

The *Cries of London* proved so popular they were extensively reprinted in recent times they have also been photographically reproduced. Value depends greatly on the date the print was made: the paper and quality of the impression are the best guide to dating. Later reprints are very muddy and dull-looking and not generally sought after. In contrast a full set of 18th-century prints is highly desirable while even early individual plates are keenly sought after.

Architecture, Travel & Topography

Early topographical views, architectural subjects, interior design and foreign scenery

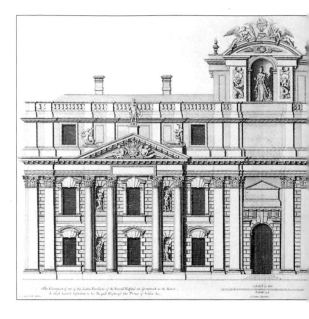

▲ Vitruvius Britannicus
The architect Colen Campbell was one of the leading 18th-century exponents of the classical style, and his Palladian designs for great houses were published in a folio entitled *Vitruvius Britannicus*. His rather tight, clinical style is less appealing than the dramatic images of Piranesi and his followers, a factor reflected in the value of this type of print. **£80–120**

Prints have long been used as a way to record and disseminate the appearance of scenery and from the earliest times printmakers made meticulous studies of landscapes, towns and buildings. Although there is some overlap between topography and landscape, topographical prints are usually distinguishable by the fact that their main aim is to record the lie of the land accurately, rather than portraying and adapting it primarily for aesthetic pleasure.

In the days before photography, when travel even across modest distances could prove difficult and hazardous, it is easy to see why there was a steady demand for prints depicting interesting domestic views, architecture and townscapes. These images now provide a fascinating and important historical record of the changing landscape and the development of towns and cities.

Interest in topographical printmaking began in northern Europe and developed hand in hand with new printmaking techniques. By the late 16th century the tradition for such scenes was well established

although the identity of most artists remains a mystery. In England, topography was a rather neglected area – most native printmakers of the 17th and 18th centuries tended to concentrate on portraiture – and many of the earliest scenes of English subjects were made by artists from Italy, Germany and France.

Interest in foreign scenery in the 18th century also created a keen demand for prints recording exotic landscapes and architecture, and as new lands were discovered and explored it became commonplace for major expeditions to include an artist to record scenery, as well as flora and fauna. On the return of such expeditions these watercolours and sketches were often worked up and published and such subject matter proved hugely popular with the public who were keen to share new discoveries and marvel at exotic scenery. The fashionable Grand Tour also inspired numerous printmakers to record the landmarks of cities such as Rome and Florence, thus providing popular souvenirs for wealthy gentlemen and their entourage. Prints also provided an important way of disseminating new architectural styles, and

▶ **After Domenico Montegu**
Veduta della Basilica e Piazza di San Pietro in Vaticano
Etchings such as this were popular souvenirs for Grand Tourists in the 18th and 19th centuries, and such architectural subjects are widely available. £150–250

◀ **Theodore Galle**
Formal Gardens, a 17th-century engraving possibly taken from a book or portfolio showing the formal style of early topographical subjects. £50–80

often proved enormously influential in shaping the taste of wealthy patrons.

As travel became easier and far-flung countries increasingly accessible during the late 18th and 19th centuries collecting prints of foreign views became more widespread. Foreign views were often published as lithographs in volumes recording the artist's travels. Among the most famous was David Roberts, whose travels to Spain, North Africa and Palestine were meticulously recorded and published on his return to wide acclaim.

The interest in prints of interiors grew along with the fascination for topography and reached a peak of popularity in the late 18th and 19th centuries. Prints of this type fall into two distinct groups: first, designer pattern books often featuring details such as draperies, chimney pieces, furniture, wallpaper and so on, and secondly views of complete interiors. The latter were avidly collected at the time they were produced and were often pasted into albums. Many of the decorative schemes depicted in prints of 18th-century interiors were inspired by discoveries of classical interiors at Herculaneum and Pompeii,

themselves popularized as prints. Prints also provided architects and designers of other decorative arts with an important means of publicizing their work. The prominent figures of the day often established their reputations by publishing their designs and in the 19th century specialist publications such as Ackermann's *Repository of the Arts* (see p35) provided a huge source of prints of the most fashionable applied arts and interiors.

Topographical prints have always been popular with collectors and today prices largely depend on the subject and on its rarity. Views of colonial Australia, the United States and India remain in particularly high demand. In contrast, prints of interiors enjoyed a huge rise in popularity in the 1980s, so much so that one auction house held special sales devoted to images of interiors. Demand now appears to have steadied although the market remains strong for interesting interiors such as royal palaces. Architectural prints achieved a similar peak of popularity in the 1980s and although prices for certain types have fallen, early prints by Piranesi and his followers remain highly sought after.

▲ **Johann Jacob Shubler**
Elaborate bed in an interior, an etching probably taken from a 17th-century pattern book. £20–30

▼ **Giovanni Battista Piranesi**
Tempio detto "Volgarm di Giano", a typically dramatic etching by Piranesi. This type of subject has been much reprinted and examples can be dated from the watermarks in the paper. £100–200

Architecture & Interiors

Architectural prints have long been considered collectable by connoisseurs and have traditionally exerted a profound influence on the spread of new architectural styles. In England in the early 18th century the most influential architectural prints were those published by the architect Colen Campbell in three volumes entitled *Vitruvius Britannicus* (1715–25). These rather clinically observed architectural designs promote the ideals of classical architecture as developed in Italy by Palladio, whom Campbell regarded as the doyen of classical taste, and played a key role in popularizing the Palladian style of architecture in Britain.

Vitruvius Britannicus contained elevations and designs by connoisseurs and professional architects such as Inigo Jones, Christopher Wren, John Vanbrugh and Nicholas Hawksmoor and included plans for country houses, palaces and public buildings, many of which were never built. Another important engraver of architectural subject matter was George Vertue who was employed by the Society of Antiquaries to make accurate records of ancient buildings. Some of Vertue's engravings were illustrated in the society's publications *Archaeologia* and *Vetusta Monumenta*; others were published individually, including the series *London Gates*, published in 1725.

On the continent one of the most outstanding and prolific architectural printmakers of the 18th century was Giovanni Battista Piranesi. Trained as an architect, Piranesi achieved huge fame with his 137 etchings of Rome, published from 1745, which became enormously popular souvenirs for Grand Tourists. Piranesi's approach to architecture was dramatic and atmospheric and in complete contrast to the rather cold clinical style of Campbell. Other publications by Piranesi include designs for chimney pieces and decorative details. Some of his most unusual etchings were the *Carceri d'Invenzione*, a series of fantastic imaginary prisons. Piranesi's success spawned several followers of his dramatic architectural style, amongst whom the best known is Luigi Rossini. Although his images are sometimes very similar to Piranesi's, Rossini often relied more on etching than engraving, frequently including detailed minuscule figures to make the scale of the architecture seem even more grand. His prints tend to sell for less than Piranesi's.

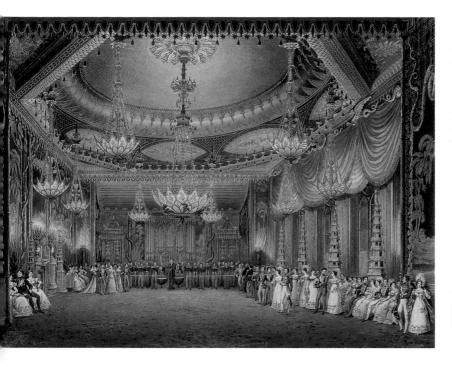

▲ **After John Nash**
One from a set of 29, taken from a series of 31 plates of the interiors of the Royal Pavilion at Brighton, published by Ackermann in 1826. This is slightly foxed but none the less highly desirable. For the set of 29: **£2,000–4,000**

Pattern books illustrating the decorative arts provided the most effective means for new fashions in interior design to be disseminated and developed alongside the fashion for topographical and architectural prints. Engravings made after the fantastic grotesques and architectural designs of Jacques Androuet Ducerceau were published in the late 16th century and provided inspiration for the applied arts of the following century.

The fashion for pattern books continued apace in the following centuries. The reputation of nearly all the most successful designers of applied arts of the 18th and 19th centuries was largely founded on the success of their printed pattern books. William Kent's opulent designs were published by John Vardy; Jean Pillement did much to fuel the appetite for *chinoiserie* by his pattern book *A New Book of Chinese Ornaments, Invented and Engraved by J. Pillement* (1755); while Robert Adam's publication of *Ruins of the Palace of the Emperor Diocletian at Spalato* introduced classical domestic architecture to an audience whose taste had, until then, largely been shaped by prints of public buildings. Continental pattern books were also highly influential and in the early 19th century, Percier and Fontaine's designs published as *Recueil de Décorations Intérieures* introduced the new Empire style to a wider audience.

Interest in fashionable interiors also spawned numerous publications showing complete room settings and proud architects commonly published prints of their completed decorative schemes. John Nash published exquisitely detailed etched and aquatint views of the Royal Pavilion finished with hand colouring, illustrating the new, opulently oriental decorative schemes by Frederick Crace and Robert Jones in 1822. Another famous series of the 19th century was Pyne's *The History of Royal Residences* (1819), a series of plates by various engravers including Thomas Sutherland, William James and others showing the recent decorations at the Royal Pavilion, Carlton House and Windsor.

Although the fashion for prints of interiors waned with the advent of photography in the 19th century, early prints provide an invaluable record of changing tastes and have long been of interest to historians. Collectors have become increasingly interested in this subject as a useful source of inspiration for furniture, upholstery and fabric design.

◀ **After Thomas Baines**
Victoria Falls, Zambesi River, published in 1865 by Day & Sons. One of a plethora of tinted, coloured lithographs of topographical views published in the 19th century, this was part of a set of ten plates, and the rare African subject matter boosts their value. **£2,500–3,000**

◀ **After Luigi Mayer**
Coloured aquatint from a series entitled *Views in the Ottoman Dominions*, published in 1810 by R. Bowyer on watermarked (and therefore datable) J. Whatman paper. These were sold as a set of 13 plates. **£200–400**

Topography

Topographical scenes became popular in the late 16th century in northern Europe. One of the most famous Continental engravers was Matthaus Merian of Frankfurt who published copious prints of European towns. Merian's best-known pupil was Wenceslaus Hollar, a prolific printmaker who was born in Prague and worked in various European centres including Frankfurt, Cologne, Stuttgart and Strasbourg. After meeting the Earl of Arundel, an English diplomat in Cologne, he accompanied him on his travels and to the Viennese court of Emperor Ferdinand II, making views of the scenery they visited. Hollar later settled in England where he made numerous etchings of English views including views of the old St Paul's Cathedral, views of Windsor Castle and fascinating panoramas of London before and after the Great Fire of 1666.

Hollar popularized the art of etching in England and followers of his meticulously accurate topographical style included Daniel King, Francis Place, Richard Gaywood and Thomas Johnson. Other important topographical printmakers of the late 17th and early 18th centuries include Johannes Kip, a Dutch etcher and engraver, whose best-known prints were made after the topographical studies of Leonard Knyff. These show bird's-eye views of great houses in their landscapes and were originally published in two volumes as *Britannia Illustrata* (1707–26), by David Mortier, a Dutch publisher. Also known by its French title *Nouveau Théâtre de la Grande Bretagne*, this was published in a four volume edition (in 1724) containing extra plates by other engravers.

The public's interest in topography grew apace in the 18th century when huge fortunes could be made publishing desirable subjects. John Boydell enjoyed notable financial success during the middle of the century by publishing views of Britain engraved from his own sketches. Publishing the work of other artists led Boydell to even greater fortune and influence, so much so that he eventually achieved the position of Lord Mayor of London.

Among the most important topographical artists in England in the 18th century were the brothers Samuel and Nathaniel Buck who made over 80 long, narrow etched panoramas of British cities and towns, often containing a key which listed prominent landmarks, or a lengthy description of the history of the buildings shown. These etchings were first published in a volume entitled *Buck's Views* and surviving examples have frequently been hand-coloured at a later date.

◄ **After Captain Richard Barron**
Views in India, Chiefly Among the Neelgherry Hills, an aquatint part-printed in colour with hand finishing, published by R. Havell in 1837. **£150–250**

► **Frank Brangwyn**
King's Lynn, etching from 1919 signed in pencil. Etchings by Brangwyn are much sought after and this richly worked composition is typical of the artist's distinctive style. **£100–200**

◄ *St Paul's Cathedral*
Etching with drypoint signed in pencil by the early 20th-century printmaker Frederick A. Farrell. London views are popular but readily available and often modestly priced. **£40–60**

Topographical prints of foreign scenery also enjoyed huge popularity in the 18th century. Thomas Daniell made lengthy expeditions to India with his 16-year-old nephew William during which they made numerous sketches of the scenery they encountered. These were worked up into aquatints and sold as two volumes entitled *Oriental Scenery* and *Views of Calcutta* (published 1786–8). William Daniell's prolific topographical output also includes aquatints after other artists as well as *Six Views of London* and *Six Views of the London Docks* (pub. in 1805), *A Voyage round Great Britain* and views of Windsor, Eton and Virginia Water, all of which were based on his own sketches.

The development of lithography in the 19th century and increasing demand for illustrated travel books spawned a host of publications featuring both well-known European scenes and far-flung exotic landscapes. Many of these scenes were made by well-known artists, whose reputation was greatly enhanced by the success of their printed works. Richard Parkes Bonington produced lithographs of northern France during his short-lived career; Samuel Prout made copious lithographs of the landscapes of France, Germany and Venice, where he worked with the artist and writer John Ruskin;

lithographs of Ruskin's drawings of Venetian architecture were produced by G. Rosenthal and published by Hanhart.

Among the most famous travellers to the East was David Roberts, whose drawings of the architecture, landscapes and peoples he encountered were lithographed by Louis Haghe and published in six volumes as *The Holy Land, Syria, Idumea, Arabia, Egypt* and *Nubia* by Day & Son (1842–9), to huge acclaim. Thomas Shotter Boys was another leading topographical artist whose career included lithographing the work of other artists, including *City and Harbour of Sydney from near Vaucluse* after G. F. Angas (1852), as well as making lithographs from his own drawings. Boys produced *Picturesque Architecture in Paris, Ghent and Antwerp* in 1839, the earliest English book with lithographic plates printed entirely in colour, from his own sketches, and his most famous work is *Original Views of London as it is* (1842).

Value for topographical views largely depends on the subject matter. Views of London, Oxford, Cambridge and other important cities are always in high demand and in recent years good early foreign views have become increasingly widely collected. West Indian views can fetch particularly high sums.

◀ **Arthur Briscoe**
Ship Building, a signed and numbered etching. Briscoe was another leading marine printmaker and artist of the early 20th century. **£100–200**

▶ **After Chris Woodhouse**
A Bristolian in Command, a modern reproduction printed in colours. Although it is signed and numbered by the artist, decorative prints of this type are of little interest to most collectors. **£30–50**

A BRISTOLIAN IN COMMAND

▲ **William Lionel Wyllie, RA**
Cobbles off Northumberland, an etching with margins signed in pencil by the artist. It is typical of his highly atmospheric subjects. **£150–250**

Marine Prints

The rise in popularity of marine prints parallels that of marine painting, since until the 20th century, the vast majority were made after paintings. Seascapes first became popular in the 17th century in the Netherlands, and artists such as Jan van de Velde II produced both paintings and etchings of marine subjects. Early marine prints are however few and far between and in Britain it was not till the early 18th century that the subject became popular.

The rise in popularity of British marine painting was largely fuelled by Britain's naval victories, and gave rise also to a noticeable increase in the numbers of prints produced. Until c.1770 prints were mostly uncoloured etchings and line engravings. Leading engravers of the early 18th century include Pierre Charles Canot, a French-born printmaker who worked in London after 1740, making etchings after the marine paintings of Dominic Serres. Benjamin Thomas Pouncy also worked around this time, producing engravings and etchings of marine subjects after Robert Cleveley. Another important engraver of the mid-18th century was Daniel Lerpiniere who

worked for the publisher Boydell and made prints after the marine paintings of Richard Paton.

Britain continued to rule the waves in the late 18th and 19th centuries and naval prowess carried on fuelling the public demand for marine subjects. Yachting scenes, picturesque shipping subjects and unusual maritime events as well as naval engagements were among a more varied repertoire of marine subjects that appeared, while aquatint replaced etching as the favoured printing technique. Robert Dodd produced aquatints after his own compositions and those of other artists; among his most famous and sought-after works are sets of four aquatints depicting the Battle of the Nile and the Victory of Trafalgar, subjects of particular interes to Admiral Nelson enthusiasts. Edward Duncan, after serving his apprenticeship under Robert Havell, made aquatints after the marine paintings of William Huggins. Printmakers only rarely used mezzotint for marine subjects, but one notable exception was Charles Turner, who capitalized on the rich inkiness of mezzotints to startling effect in his prints of the dramatic stormy seascapes of

▲ **Robert Dodd**
The Mutineers turning Lieut. Bligh with some of the Officers and Crew adrift from His Majesty's Ship the Bounty, an aquatint with etching on laid paper.
£1,000–2,000

▶ **After Thomas Whitcombe,**
The Battle of Camperdowne by T. Hellyer. A coloured mixed-method engraving originally published in 1799 by B. B. Evans. This is a mid-19th-century reprint, and therefore much less valuable. **£100–200**

J. M. W. Turner. His first mezzotint after Turner was entitled *A Shipwreck* and published in 1805.

Lithography was also a popular medium for reproducing prints of marine subjects from the mid-19th century. Thomas Goldsworth Dutton is best-known for his tinted lithographs, some with hand colouring, after the works of Oswald Walter Brierly; many of his prints were published by Rudolph Ackermann. Joseph Needham also produced lithographs after Brierly. Other 19th-century lithographers of marine subjects include John R. Isaacs, who made prints of shipping in Liverpool, and G. P. Reinagle.

The sea and marine subjects continued to inspire printmakers of the later 19th and 20th centuries. The American artist James Abbott McNeill Whistler produced etchings with drypoint and lithotints (a type of lithography) depicting scenes of shipping on the Thames. One of the most prolific marine printmakers was William Lionel Wyllie RA, who made highly atmospheric, rather sketchy etchings and drypoints of shipping, some of which were published by Robert Dunthorne. Wyllie also produced shipping posters for the Orient Company, Union Castle and White Star Lines (see pp112–13). Ship building and the sea were also recurring themes that captivated the artist Frank Brangwyn.

Though popular with collectors, marine prints are far less common than other collecting areas, such as sporting or genre prints, and perhaps for this reason at the larger auction houses they are often sold in specialist sales of marine art rather than general print sales. Prices invariably reflect steady demand but many of the most famous early prints have been reprinted at a later date and earlier impressions of good quality will command a far higher price than later ones. Good early impressions of Charles Turner's mezzotints after J. M. W. Turner are highly priced, as are etchings by eminent late 19th- and early 20th-century artists such as Brangwyn, Wyllie and Whistler. The popular demand for colourful marine subjects is such that numerous modern colour reproductions are also seen on the market; even if signed in pencil and numbered by the artists these generally fetch small sums and would have little resale value.

◄ **Robert Morden**

Maps such as this of Cambridgeshire – made to illustrate *Camden's Britannia* in 1695 – are less valuable than those by John Speed of the same date because they are less decorative.
£70–100

► **Christopher Saxton**

Saxton maps first published in the 16th century were much reprinted and the best are lavishly decorated. This map of Lancashire from 1577 is relatively plain and is also damaged, although the galleon and other details add to its appeal. **£600–800**

Maps

Maps have been made since ancient times but the majority of those you are likely to come across today were made from the 16th century onwards. Age, rarity and decorative appeal all have an important bearing on the value of maps. Early maps of America, the Far East and Australasia are far rarer than those of Europe and therefore often attract particularly high prices. Decorative details such as sea monsters, elaborate cartouches, sailing ships, landscape vignettes and heraldic emblems are also often found on early maps and will add to the value of less rare subjects. Many of the most famous early maps have been much reprinted throughout the centuries and as with other types of print, early strong impressions are far more valuable and desirable than later ones.

Exploration, the improvement of measuring instruments and advances in printing techniques all played a part in the development of European mapping in the 15th and 16th centuries. The earliest printed maps were woodcuts but gradually engrav-

ing, which allowed for greater detail, became the favoured method of printing. Maps were printed in black and white and often sold either with hand colouring or (less expensively) plain. Some originally plain maps have been coloured at a later date and these are less desirable than those with original colour. Nearly all early maps were originally sold bound in books but in many cases these have since been broken up to be sold individually.

Among the most famous early cartographers was the Flemish map-maker Gerard Mercator who was the first to show the parallels and meridians at a uniform 90-degree angle. Mercator published a famous atlas between c.1585 and 1595 which appeared in many different editions. In England, Christopher Saxton was the first to survey England and Wales accurately in the 1570s. Saxton's maps were copper plate engraved with hand colouring. Earlier maps of England, such as the one by Mercator, invariably showed English place names in Latin or other languages (depending on the nation-

▼ Maitland's *History of London*

Map of Langborn Ward, a London Parish by B. Cole, 1755. Though this map is rather too plain to attract most collectors, it might have limited local appeal. **£60–80**

▲ John Speed

This decorative map of Cornwall (1611) is typically decorated with heraldic emblems and an attractive vignette. **£300–500**

► Georg Matthaus Seutter

This 18th-century map of the British Isles was produced by a German cartographer from a well-known family. Though the map is small, the subject has wide appeal. **£100–200**

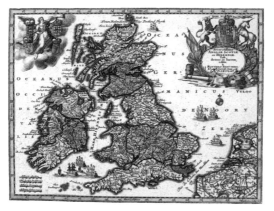

ality of the cartographer); Saxton was the first to print place names in English. Saxton's map of England was adapted by many other cartographers such as John Speed, Johannes Blaeu and Johannes Jansson. His own maps also enjoyed huge popularity and were reprinted throughout the 17th and 18th centuries, though sometimes reduced in size. The best Saxtons are very richly decorated and heightened with gilt and decorative details such as cartouches and galleons; they remain much sought after by collectors.

In the 17th century Holland dominated overseas trade and exploration, and in the production of maps the Dutch were similarly preeminent, with cartographers such as Blaeu and Jansson famed throughout Europe. Although Dutch maps were extensively sold in England, sometimes with English text, Speed's maps replaced those of Saxton as the most detailed and accurate English-made maps of the century. Speed's maps, published c.1610, included town plans, heraldic emblems and

topographical vignettes and are extremely popular with collectors for their decorative appeal. Such was the demand that Speed maps were reissued until the end of the 18th century; photographic reproductions have also been made in the 20th century. Until the third quarter of the 17th century few maps in England showed roads, and it was not until 1675, with the publication of John Ogilby's *Britannica*, that roads were a regular feature.

As travel became easier in the 18th and 19th centuries numerous small country atlases, maps and traveller's companions were mass-produced. Among the best known are those by John Owen and Emanuel Bowen, John Senex, Thomas Jeffreys, Daniel Paterson and the publisher Carington Bowles. With the evolution of lithography, colour printing replaced hand colouring.

Most 19th-century maps of Europe are of little value to collectors, but if the map is of an interesting location they may still fetch high sums. A mid-19th-century map of New York recently sold for £8,000.

Sporting Prints

Hunting, racing, coaching and other sporting subjects

▲ **Carington Bowles**
A Soft Tumble After a Hard Ride, a hand-coloured mezzotint published 1779. The publisher Carington Bowles specialized in comical sporting subjects such as this with rather bright colouring; many were sold in series and are numbered. This is one of a pair estimated at **£300–400**.

Sporting prints are among the most perennially popular subjects and despite the fact that almost all those seen are of English origin their popularity extends to America and Europe. English printmakers dominated the market for sporting prints and the golden age for such subjects was the late 18th and 19th centuries, when vast quantities were produced. The range of sports covered by antique prints is extremely varied and includes now obsolete pastimes such as cock fighting, rat hunting and bear baiting as well as wrestling and boxing, ballooning, angling, tennis, golf and cricket. Equestrian sports include racing, hunting and steeple chasing.

By far the largest proportion of prints that survive today relate to equestrian sports. This is a reflection not only of the enormous popularity of hunting and racing at the time, but also of the fact that these pastimes tended to be practised by the more affluent sections of the population – the people who could afford to buy good-quality prints.

To the print-buying public of the 18th and 19th centuries sporting prints performed several different functions. Some were made as "news" items, recording a memorable sporting event: a prize-fighter's victory, a win at the Derby, a memorable balloon flight. Some were humorous in intent, and poked fun at the conventions of the various sports, their participators and spectators. Others, often those made after the paintings of leading sporting artists, were produced as a way of publicizing the artist's work, and catered to the huge public demand for such subjects.

Although prints of sports such as golf, tennis, cricket and angling survive in relatively limited quantities, prints of equestrian sports are still readily available today. Numerous reprints were made of the most popular subjects and prices vary considerably according to age, quality and

▼ **After Harry Hall**
The Merry Beaglers, an aquatint with engraving by J. Harris, originally published in 1848 by J. Watson. Traditional sporting subjects such as this are always popular with collectors. **£200–400**

condition. The modern distaste for blood sports means that some collectors are becoming more fastidious about buying gruesome hunting scenes, although prices for good early hunting prints, especially appealing ones, are still strong. Prints of sports that are still played today such as tennis, golf and angling tend to be collected by enthusiasts of the sport rather than by general print collectors. For this reason at auction they are often sold in specialist sporting sales rather than in general print sales, and good early prints showing the most popular sports always command a premium.

Most early scenes were produced as black and white engravings or mezzotints, but hand-coloured sporting scenes were made from the second half of the 18th century, and original colour always adds to the value of the most sought-after subjects.

By the last decades of the 18th century hand-coloured aquatints, some part-printed in colour (usually blue and brown), were produced. Lithographs of sporting subjects continued to be made in the 19th century. Equestrian subjects were often sold in sets, generally of four to eight plates, and prices varied according to the quality of the paper, the size and whether or not the image was coloured. Today prices are also affected by how close to the original publication date the image was printed.

In the 20th century the demand for works by leading sporting artists such as "Snaffles" (Charles Johnson Payne) and Lionel Edwards has led to the publication of photographic reproductions of their work in signed editions or in editions stamped with the artist's blind stamp (in the case of Snaffles editions). Although photographic reproductions are not generally considered desirable by serious print collectors, hand-signed editions by certain eminent figures are occasionally of interest to sporting enthusiasts.

▼ **After Lionel Edwards**
A reproduction printed in colour, signed in pencil by the artist and published by Eyre & Spottiswoode. Reproductions of paintings such as this are not generally sought after unless they are signed by hand and by a leading artist such as Edwards. This was one of a portfolio of nine prints. **£200–300** for the set.

▲ **After Walter Parry Hodges**
First published by T. McLean in 1834, this hand-coloured aquatint *The Cocktails Done* can be dated to around 1850 by the J. Whatman Turkey Mill papermark. **£100–200**

Equestrian Prints

To an 18th-century gentleman a portrait of his horse was nearly as essential as a portrait of himself and his family, and the popularity of equestrian sporting prints made in England in the late 18th and 19th centuries reflects the national preoccupation with horses, as well as the growing popularity of country pursuits such as fox hunting, steeple chasing and racing.

Nearly all sporting prints were made after paintings by leading equestrian artists. Early in the 18th century paintings by artists such as Peter Tillemans and John Wootton were reproduced as engravings or mezzotints. Subjects typically showed the favourite horses belonging to wealthy aristocrats and invariably included a lengthy inscription detailing the name of the illustrious owner and the horse's ancestry. In the second half of the century prints were made after painters such as James Seymour, George Stubbs, John and his son Francis Sartorius, Robert Houston, John William Edy and others.

The Jockey Club, which regulated famous racing meetings, was founded in 1750 and from this date onwards prints depicting champion racehorses, exciting racing events, or views of meetings were made in increasing numbers. Prints after James

Seymour's racing and hunting scenes were first published in 1753 a year after his death. Aquatints of racing subjects also began to appear in the middle of the 18th century; among the earliest examples are prints after Francis Sartorius.

The leading painter George Stubbs also published prints of his paintings of champion racehorses engraved by his son George Townley Stubbs, as well as shooting subjects engraved by William Woollet (published 1771). Stubbs' technical and anatomical accuracy was far ahead of his contemporaries, and his mezzotints and engravings are highly sought after by collectors.

Sporting prints were sold as separate sheets, in folios or as illustrations for books, many of which have been taken out at a later date. Many images enjoyed huge popularity for years after their first publication and they are particularly prone to reprinting. Value can therefore vary significantly according to the date the print was published and the quality of the impression.

Among the most amusing sporting prints of the 18th century are those published by Carington Bowles or Bowles & Carver. These mezzotints by unknown artists were garishly coloured by hand in

▶ After James Pollard
This hand-coloured aquatint, *Royal Hunt in Windsor Park*, was first published in 1820 by E. Orme. It is in poor condition but the subject – George III out hunting – enhances the value. **£100–150**

▲ **Charles Hunt**
Cheltenham Annual Grand Steeplechase, an aquatint published by I. W. Laird, sold in a set of four. **£300–400** for the set

▶ After Walter Parry Hodges Originally published in 1833, this version of *The Beaufort Hunt*, published by T. McLean on wove paper probably dates from later in the century. **£120–150**

gouache, and show scenes such as revellers travelling to or returning from a day at the races. Unlike many sporting prints which were sold in folios, they were intended to be treated as paintings and hung on a wall and are often seen still in their original 18th-century frames.

The demand for prints of sporting subjects peaked in the 19th century, and prints were increasingly made using aquatint and later lithography. Samuel Howitt, Thomas Rowlandson's brother-in-law, was a leading sporting printmaker from the early 19th century. Howitt produced designs for plates, illustrating *British Field Sports* (1807–8), *The British Sportsman* (1799–1800) and *Oriental Field Sports* (1807).

Famous racehorses continued to be recorded in print throughout the 19th century. James Ward produced 14 lithographs entitled *Celebrated Horses*. These were first published 1823–4 at prices ranging from ten guineas to eight shillings, depending on whether the edition was hand-coloured or black and white, and showed the horse concerned against a rather romanticized setting. Prints were also produced after John Frederick Herring's paintings of St Leger winners from 1815–43.

Nearly all the leading print publishers of the 19th century were keen to cash in on the booming market for racing and sporting subjects. Rudolph Ackermann published a series of *National Races* in 1847 and other leading specialist publishers included S. & J. Fuller, whose shop called "The Sporting Gallery" bore testimony to the lucrative market in such material.

The most prolific of sporting artists of the 19th century were undoubtedly James Pollard (see also p69) and Henry Alken, both of whom produced vast quantities of sporting prints in the first quarter of the 18th century. Henry Alken was the son of Samuel Alken and father of Samuel Henry Alken. They all produced sporting prints, though Henry was by far the most prolific. His early prints were published under the name of Ben Tally-Ho, although he reverted to his real name later in his career. Alken's prints were often produced in sets with some series containing up to 40 plates and bookplates. The most famous, and today highly sought-after, examples of his work are his sets of the Beaufort and Quorn hunts, published in 1833 and 1835, but as with most well-loved sporting prints, these have been extensively reprinted.

▼ ► **After Charles Cooper Henderson**
Plates I and II in a series entitled *Fores Coaching Recollections*, coloured aquatints by J. Harris, published 1842 by Fores.
£300–500 for the pair

Coaching Scenes

The bustle of departing mails leaving London for their evening run; stagecoach journeys under way with coaches travelling at full speed; stops along the road; the problems encountered along the way; inclement weather; horses shying at some unexpected hazard; broken carriage wheels – all are lovingly depicted in printed form in the plethora of coaching prints that date from the late 18th to the mid-19th century. At this time coaching was still the main method of transport, and it is not therefore surprising that the stagecoach, which transported people, letters and news, should have preoccupied artists and printmakers to such an extent. Even after the coach had been replaced by the steam train as the most efficient method of transport, coaching scenes continued to evoke enormous public nostalgia, but although they remained popular and were reprinted during the 19th century, the artists who made a living from depicting them, such as Pollard and Alken, declined in popularity. Both died in poverty despite the enormous success they had enjoyed in the golden age of coaching scenes: the first three decades of the century.

Coaching scenes provide a fascinating insight into the trials, achievements and spectacles this method of transport involved. Prints were made to show topical events such as journeys achieved in record time, last runs of famous mail coaches, or the King's birthday, when the royal mail coaches paraded to St James's Palace. The hierarchy of transport by coach is also reflected in these prints. Only the most affluent could afford to belong to the

FORES'S SPORTING TRAPS.

GOING TO COVER.

◄ After Henry Alken
Alken was one of the most popular sporting artists. This aquatint entitled *Return from the Derby* was engraved by W. Summers and is typical of his action-packed compositions. **£150–200**

▲ After Charles Cooper Henderson
Going to Cover, a coloured aquatint by J. Harris, was published in 1847 in a series entitled *Fores Sporting Traps* by Messrs Fores, a leading print publisher of the day. **£150–200**

exclusive "Four in Hand" club (a four in hand was a privately owned coach); most well-to-do people travelled on the stagecoach, or, if they were in a hurry on the royal mail coach – the fastest method of transport at the time but also the most expensive.

By far the most prolific artist of coaching scenes was James Pollard (1797–1867) whose minutely observed details of coaches and the people who drove them, serviced them and travelled in them are packed into every scene. Pollard was born in Clerkenwell and began his career painting inn signs. He reproduced few of his paintings as aquatints himself but most were done by specialists such as Theodore Henry Adolphus Fielding, Charles Rosenberg I and II, and Frederick and Richard Rosenberg. Aquatints by his own hand have a distinctively coarse granular appearance but are very rare. Most of Pollard's work was part-printed in blue and brown and finished with hand colouring. Early impressions were on J. Whatman paper and are much sought after, but the many reprints on the market, identifiable by the later paper or even a reduction in size, are far less desirable.

Other leading artists of coaching scenes include Pollard's contemporàry Henry Alken (see p67), and Charles Cooper Henderson, whose coaching scenes, published by Fores in several famous series including *Fores Coaching Recollections* (1842) and *Fores Sporting Traps* (published 1847), were more dramatic than Pollard's and managed to remain popular with collectors long after coaches had become obsolete as a means of transport.

▼ **After Francis Hayman**
Engraving by C. Grignon of the lost painting by
Hayman. Early cricketing subjects such as this
are rare and much sought after. **£300–500**

▲ **After Robert Smirke and John Emes**
*The Society of Royal British Archers in
Gwersyllt Park, Denbighshire*, an aquatint
with etching by C. Apostool, published
1794. Despite the surface dirt and damage
this is an interesting subject. **£300–500**

Other Sporting Prints

The plethora of sports which were represented in the form of prints provide a fascinating record of how games evolved, and reflect the changing fashions in sporting pursuits. Among the various sports to which printmakers turned their attentions were archery, ballooning, boxing, skating, tennis, rackets and shuttlecock, croquet, golf, football, angling, fencing, yachting, rowing, bear baiting and even rat hunting. Since early sporting prints were often produced as newsworthy items rather than as "art" many were unsigned and the absence of an artist's name tends to have little effect on the value of rarer sporting subjects. Although good early prints are increasingly rare and valuable, sporting prints have continued to be produced in considerable quantity in the late 19th and 20th centuries, and many of these are still fairly readily available at accessible prices.

Boxing and wrestling were among the most popular of sports in the 18th and 19th centuries, and a great number of pugilistic prints were produced to record landmark fights, interesting incidents or celebrated prize fighters. Among the famous characters whose feats are immortalized in prints were prize fighters such as Tom Cribb, Thomas Belcher, Richard Humphreys, Daniel Mendoza and John "Gentleman" Jackson, one of the most famous of all early heavyweights. Most of these prints were intended for the mass market and were printed on inexpensive paper, and as a result relatively few survive, considering the numbers in which they were originally produced.

Cock fighting was another popular sport which inspired numerous prints throughout the 18th and 19th centuries. William Hogarth published a famous engraving entitled *The Cockpit*, showing the rapacious audience at a London cockfight in Birdcage Walk, which was built by Henry VIII and finally closed in 1816. Cock fighting was not outlawed until 1849 and prints continued to be disseminated throughout the first half of the century.

Ballooning also became a popular spectator sport in the late 18th century and prints were made to record notable flights in France and England, such as the 1783 trip of Charles and Roberts from the Tuileries gardens in Paris. Early flights were also recorded by Jean-François Rigaud and translated into stipple by Francesco Bartolozzi, and the public's fascination with hot-air balloons was also humorously interpreted by caricaturists of the age.

Cricket was only occasionally recorded by early printmakers, but one of the most famous early paintings of the sport was by Francis Hayman for a supper box in Vauxhall Gardens. This now lost painting is known only by engravings, which provide an important record of the game's early

▶ After Philip Reinagle
Coloured aquatint published 1810 by C. Random. *Roebuck Shooting* is typical of the sporting subjects that remained popular throughout the 19th century. **£200–400**

▼ After W. Gauci
One of a pair of coloured lithographs from *A. F. Rolfe's Angling Scenes: Salmon Fishing* published 1857 by W. Tegg & Co. **£800–1,000** for the pair

◀ After Edmund Havell
View of Reading School and Playground, a 19th-century hand-coloured aquatint by R. Havell depicting a cricket match. **£300–500**

evolution. Other early printmakers of cricketing subjects include Isaac Robert Cruikshank and Thomas Rowlandson.

Among the most popular sporting prints with today's collectors are golfing subjects. Golfing prints were published from the late 18th century. One of the earliest golf prints dates from 1790, and showed a portrait of William Innes, Captain of the Society of Golfers at Blackheath, after a portrait by Lemuel Francis Abbot. This was first published as a mezzotint by Valentine Green and numerous reprints of the original edition of 50 have been made. Among the best-known sporting artists who depicted golf (and other sports) are Cecil Aldin, John Hassall, Victor Venner and Lionel Edwards.

Many of the sporting prints that survive were produced originally as illustrations for books or magazines. Angling books enjoyed particular popularity and among the earliest subjects were Francis Barlow's engravings for *Gentleman's Recreation*; Johan Zoffany and Samuel Howitt also recorded the details of this popular sport. One of the most famous early sporting books was *British Sportsman* published in 1800 with 72 engravings by Samuel Howitt of various sporting pursuits. Several sporting books detailing different country pastimes were written by "Nimrod", (Charles James Appleby) with illustrations by Henry Alken, while publications such as

Life in London included scenes of cock fighting, boxing and fencing. Later in the 19th century sport continued to be a popular theme for printmakers, and William Nicholson, an accomplished maker of colour wood blocks, illustrated *An Almanac of Sports*, a calendar illustrated with a different sport for each month of the year.

Humorous sporting prints are also enduringly popular with collectors and have been produced since the 18th century. Thomas Rowlandson's satirical repertoire included sporting subjects such as boxing, cricket and ballooning, and in the 19th century, artists such as Henry Mayo Bateman and William Heath Robinson also produced tongue-in-cheek cartoons of sporting scenes. Photographic reproductions of their work are seen on the market but are generally of low value.

Unlike other print collecting areas, the growing demand for good sporting subjects by well-known artists has led to increasing numbers of 20th-century prints being reproduced photographically and individually signed by the artist. The value of these relies on the reputation of the artist concerned and the availability of original works and prints. Some well-known artists produced few original prints and, in these cases, individually signed photographically reproduced prints are often regarded as collectable, although still modestly priced.

Natural History

Illustrations of plants, birds and animals from medieval times to the present day

▲ After Joseph Dalton Hooker

A plate from *Illustrations of Himalayan Plants* (1855), a series of coloured lithographs by W. H. Fitch and one of the most famous publications of the 19th century. For a set of 24: **£1,000–3,000**

Animals, birds and plants are among the earliest of printed images. Bestiaries in which mythological animals such as dragons and unicorns were illustrated alongside real ones served to establish man's status within the natural hierarchy, and proliferated throughout the Middle Ages. Herbals, the earliest books with detailed but primitive illustrations of plants, disseminated medicinal knowledge. Over the following centuries growing interest in science, exploration and discovery led to increasing emphasis being placed upon the accuracy with which plants and animals were depicted. As new printing techniques were developed it became possible to portray the natural world in startling detail and prints played a fundamental role in the discovery and spread of knowledge about new species of animals, birds and plants.

Nowadays the use of photographic illustrations has supplanted printmaking as a way of recording interesting natural phenomena, but prints of such subjects remain of interest both for their historic content and aesthetic appeal. Natural history subjects have, ever since the 18th century, also been appreciated for their decorative appeal; in recent years this trend has enjoyed a revival and they are frequently seen fashionably mounted and framed in print galleries.

However, the vast majority of prints of botanical and zoological subjects seen on the market today were not originally made to be displayed in this way at all, but were intended as illustrations for books, magazines or folios for specialists and amateur enthusiasts. Individual prints dating from before the 18th century are rare, although unidentified woodcuts are occasionally seen in print auctions, many stuck into albums, and are often very affordable. Most natural history prints date from the 19th century, when huge numbers of such publications were produced.

Among the most sought-after botanical and zoological subjects are plates from the leading publications of the 19th century. These include works by eminent artists and publishers such as Audubon, Gould, Thornton and Redouté. Unfortunately the popularity of these major names has led to increasing numbers of photographic

▲ **After William Shiels
and William Nicholson**
Old English Breed, a
coloured lithograph by
T. Fairland published in
*Breeds of the Domestic
Animals of the British
Islands.* **£100–200**

◄ **After D. Diderot**
Kakaloes and other birds, an
etching with later colouring on
laid paper, is a typical example
of 18th-century decorative
ornithological prints. **£30–50**

reproductions being produced. Photographic
reprints of works that were originally printed
by another method such as lithography,
mezzotint, stipple engraving or aquatint
are not generally desirable to print collectors.
Exceptions to this rule are prints by major
20th-century artists such as Archibald
Thorburn and David Shepherd; the
reputations of these artists are such that
hand-signed photographic reproductions
of their work are collected.

Although major names such as Audubon
and Gould now attract very substantial prices,
it is still possible to form a highly decorative
collection of botanical or natural history prints
by buying at auction. Print sales often contain
large unframed lots of prints originally taken
from magazines and books, for a fraction of
the price you would pay a dealer for a set of
framed and mounted prints, although the
cost of framing must be taken into account.

Not all natural history prints were made
for scientific purposes. Some flower prints
were made originally as illustrations for
seed catalogues and were intended to show
keen gardeners the range of plants that was

available. Robert Furber, who ran a nursery
in London, commissioned the famous Dutch
flower painter Peter Casteels to draw plates
for the months of the year as a catalogue for
his business. Every plate was a complex
arrangement of the flowers which bloomed in
that month and which could be bought from
Furber's establishment. Flower painting was
also traditionally considered a suitable pastime
for ladies, and books containing prints were
published to be copied as part of a young
woman's education. Books of birds were also
published in which coloured prints faced the
same image in black and white so the owner
could hand-colour them using the guide
provided – the origin of some of the less
accomplished later coloured prints seen today.

Unless the print comes from one of the
leading publications, value depends largely
on the size and visual appeal of the subject. A
large colourful print of a bird of paradise will
invariably fetch more than a drab sparrow,
although the field is so diverse that even
collectors who are interested in more obscure
subjects such as reptiles, shells or insects will
almost certainly find plenty to fascinate them.

▲ After Pierre-Joseph Redouté
An 18th-century engraving after
Redouté. Because this example has
been coloured at a later date the
value is reduced. **£80–120**

**► The Magazine of
Botany**
A coloured etching after
Sir Joseph Paxton, one
of a series of 128 plates
taken from a periodical
that would sell unframed
for **£600–800**.

◄ Temple of Flora
The Dragon Arum, one of
a series of mezzotints first
published by Dr Robert
Thornton in 1801. The
lily, shown against a
characteristically dramatic
background with an
exploding volcano, was
painted by Henderson and
engraved by William Ward.
£300–500

Botanical Prints

Prints of plants and flowers have long fascinated collectors both for their botanical interest and their visual charm. Like other natural history subjects, nearly all botanical prints seen on the general market today have been removed from books or periodicals or were produced as part of a portfolio. The most collectable tend to be those that were produced in portfolios and were specially commissioned. These were often expensively produced on high-quality paper with a sheet listing the names of the original subscribers on the front.

The earliest prints of plants and flowers date from the 15th century and were made as illustrations for herbals: books detailing the medicinal properties of plants. The specimens in these early prints tended to be very formally drawn, often copied from other sources rather than drawn from life, and as a result bear little resemblance to the actual plant. Most herbals were illustrated using the woodblock method of printing, sometimes coloured by hand, or left blank for buyers to colour in at their leisure. Some early botanical subjects were also printed to provide patterns for the needlework and samplers with which ladies of the day occupied much of their time.

Prints with botanical subject matter flourished in the 17th century when the increasing interest in gardens and fashion for creating collections of rare imported plants fuelled the demand both for flower painting and for printed books detailing rare speci-

mens. By this date engraving and etching had largely replaced woodcuts as the preferred method of printing, and drawings became increasingly naturalistic and finely observed. One of the outstanding early botanical illustrators was Nicholas Robert, who was appointed royal miniature painter to the French King Louis XIV, and whose engraved illustrations of flowers were some of the most accomplished of the period.

During the 18th century botanical prints became increasingly decorative. Famous publications from this time include Robert Furber's *Twelve Months of Flowers*, which was in fact intended as a catalogue for plants – Furber ran a nursery in Kensington. The plants were shown in large elaborate mixed arrangements and the visual appeal of these hand-coloured mezzotints has meant that they have frequently been reprinted.

The most famous botanical artist of the mid-18th century, whose works were engraved to illustrate numerous books on botany and travel, was Georg Dionysius Ehret. Ehret was born in Heidelberg in Germany, the son of a gardener whose father taught him to draw. After following in his father's footsteps and training as a gardener Ehret found that his increasing proficiency as an illustrator inspired him to travel throughout Europe, drawing many of the flowers he saw. Ehret eventually settled in England where he enjoyed

▶ **Sir Joseph Dalton Hooker**
Hooker (1817–1911), son of the botanical artist William Hooker, was editor of *The Botanical Magazine* (1787–1983), the most important botanical periodical. This coloured lithograph, *The Rhododendrons of Sikkim-Himalaya* was published in 1849. **£100–200**

▲ **Henry C. Andrews**
Erica Primula, a coloured engraving from 38 volumes, each containing three plates, published 1802–9. For the set: **£1,500–2,000**

huge success not only as an illustrator but also as a drawing instructor to ladies of the leisured classes.

Another artist whose work dominated the later 18th and early 19th centuries and whose name is now synonymous with botanical illustration was Pierre-Joseph Redouté. The son of a Belgian artist, Redouté became renowned for the illustrations he made of the large plant collection assembled by Joséphine Bonaparte at her country residence, the Château de Malmaison. Redouté's illustrations were reproduced using colour stipple engraving, a method of printing rarely used for botanical subjects in England at this time but which he found ideally suited to reproduce subtle gradations of tone. Both Ehret and Redouté have enjoyed such fame that their works have been extensively reprinted since first publication and collectors need to examine both the image and the paper carefully to ensure authenticity, as later reprints are worth a fraction of the price of an original.

The interest in scientific exploration also led to the publication of increasing numbers of exotic botanical prints. Sir Joseph Banks the celebrated naturalist patronized the German artists Francis and Ferdinand Bauer, employing Francis as draughtsman to the Royal Gardens at Kew while his brother joined Matthew Flinders' expedition to Australia. Many of their highly accomplished botanical studies were published as hand-coloured engravings.

Perhaps the most visually impressive of all botanical subjects is the series of prints known as Thornton's *Temple of Flora*. This eye-catching series of around 30 plates was published between 1798 and 1812 by Robert John Thornton, a London doctor with a passion for botany. Thornton commissioned prominent artists of the day, such as Philip Reinagle, Abraham Pether, John Russell and Peter Charles Henderson, many of whom had little or no training in botanical drawing, and used leading engravers such as Francesco Bartolozzi, Richard Cooper and Richard Earlom to transfer their work onto copper. The flowers were shown drawn against dramatic backgrounds. Prints from Thornton's folio are keenly collected and prices for most range from £300–500.

As the 19th century progressed the development of lithography and chromolithography transformed the illustration of botanical subject matter which could be more easily and effectively printed in colour using the new methods. Numerous periodicals and books were published at this time and many of the plates seen in sale rooms and galleries taken from such publications have little status as collectables, although they are often highly decorative. At auction it is often possible to buy such material in multiple lots unframed for £10–100 per plate, and this can provide an ideal way for a novice buyer to establish a collection.

◀ **Herbert Dicksee**
The Tiger, an etching with aquatint published 1900 by Frost & Reed, shows a more romantic approach to the subject. **£300–500**

▶ **French School, 18th-century**
Small animal plates such as this have usually been taken from books but are fairly popular with collectors, especially if they are bizarre. This is typical of the animal subjects often found pasted in scrapbooks and albums. **£20–50**

Birds & Animals

Animals and birds have inspired artists and print-makers from the earliest times. One of the most influential sources of inspiration for applied arts in medieval times was the bestiary – a picture book containing images of animals and fictitious monsters each imbued with moral significance. The gap between such fantastic images and a more scientific approach to the subject was first bridged in the 16th century by Conrad Gessner, a Swiss-born artist whose most famous work, the *Historia Animalium*, attempted to observe and record animals more accurately.

As science became a fashionable pastime for the educated members of society in the 17th century, interest in books that detailed and described animals and birds flourished. Major publications include *Ornithologiae* by Ulyssis Aldrovandi: three volumes published in Bologna in 1603 illustrated with wood-cuts. In London Francis Willughby published his *Ornithologiae* in 1678, an important book in which the birds, illustrated with engravings, were classified by type rather than the countries in which they were found. As the passion for exploration grew in the 18th century, books and prints played an important role in making known the discovery and documentation of new species. Major expeditions usually included an artist, or an accomplished crew member, whose sketches would be worked up and reproduced as prints on their return.

In France the fascination for charting the wonders of the natural world was equally fervent.

Daubenton's *Planches Enluminées* was a folio of hand-coloured engravings mostly of birds after drawings by Martinet. Published in 1765–81, the plates were originally intended as illustrations for another gargantuan publication, Buffon's *Histoire Naturelle Générale* (completed in 1804).

In England leading artists included George Edwards, whose book *The Natural History of Uncommon Birds* (published 1743–64) was much reprinted; and his friend Mark Catesby, who produced prints of crustacea and fish as well as animals and birds. Another leading natural history specialist, whose work has been much reprinted and can be bought affordably, was Thomas Bewick. Technically, Bewick is important for his pivotal role in reviving interest in wood engraving and many of the animals and birds featured in *A History of British Birds*, published in 1797–1804, and *A General History of Quadrupeds* were based on his own observations.

The 19th century saw a huge increase in the number of lavishly illustrated folios of bird prints. Today plates from these publications are among the most desirable of all bird prints. One of the most famous bird artists was John James Audubon, whose book *Birds of America* has become an ornithological landmark. The illegitimate son of a French trader and his Creole mistress, Audubon worked as a taxidermist and hunter in America where he began to produce a series of life-size illustrations of the birds he saw. Having failed to find an American

Collecting
John Gould Birds

▲ **John Gould & H. C. Richter**
Formosan Spotted Woodpecker, a coloured lithograph published by Walter & Cohn. **£200–400**

publisher for his work, Audubon came to England and his 435 studies were converted into aquatints by Robert Havell (published 1827–38). He later published *Quadrupeds of America* (1842–5), but his studies of birds remain the most highly acclaimed of his works and have been much reprinted and reproduced in later years.

The 19th century also saw a dramatic increase in interest in exotic and foreign birds. Edward Lear's folio of 42 lithographic plates of *The Family of Psittacidae or Parrots*, published in 1832, was, he claimed, the first to be devoted to a single species. These studies were also probably the first to be made from live subjects. (Audubon worked from dead birds, which he wired to make them look alive.)

Birds and animals have continued to be a source of interest to artists and printmakers of the 20th century. Hand-signed photographic reproductions of game birds by Archibald Thorburn are popular with collectors, but do not usually fetch high prices at auction. Charles Tunnicliffe produced some charming wood engravings of farm animals (see p18); pigs and cows are particularly popular.

The interest in protecting endangered species has also fuelled a demand for animal subjects. Signed photographic reproductions of paintings of African animals and other wildlife subjects by David Shepherd, published by Soloman & Whitehead, are also increasingly sought after, and can often bought very affordably at auction.

One of the most financially successful of the ornithological printmakers was John Gould, whose famous publications include *The Birds of Europe* (1832–7), *The Birds of Australia* (1837–8), and *The Birds of Great Britain* (1862–73). Although known as "Gould" prints, most of the illustrations in these volumes were in fact drawn by different artists and reproduced as coloured lithographs by his wife, Elizabeth Gould, and other printmaking specialists. Gould employed many of the leading bird artists of the day including Joseph Wolf, H. C. Richter, W. Hart and Edward Lear. Among his most desirable lithographs are those of Australian birds which tend to be more sought after and twice as valuable as less "exotic" species from Britain and Europe. Novice collectors should be aware, however, that photographic reproductions of John Gould lithographs sometimes appear on the market, although these are usually easily identifiable by the type of paper on which they are printed.

Fashion, Costume & Design

Illustrations of dress, from images of regional costumes to fashion plates from magazines

Prints of fashion and costume have throughout the centuries performed two main functions: first, satisfying public curiosity about the costumes and clothes of people from foreign lands, and second, facilitating the spread of changes in fashionable dress, by providing information on new trends and designs.

The origins of the fashion plate can be traced back to the 16th century when illustrations of regional costumes were made in response to public curiosity about customs in other European countries. In the 17th century, volumes containing costume illustrations were among the prolific engravings published by Wenceslaus Hollar. One of his most interesting early publications, published in 1636, entitled *Ornatus Muliebris*, or the *Severall Habits of English Women, from the Nobilitie to the Country Woman as they are in these times*, contained a series of 26 plates showing a range of costumes in styles made familiar in the fashionable paintings of

Antony van Dyck and his contemporaries.

Hollar's other notable costume subjects include series of figures dressed according to the seasons of the year; a volume of European women's costumes with 100 plates entitled *Theatrum Mulierum*; and a small series of plates illustrating meticulously observed fur muffs, published in 1642. All these prints are packed with incredibly intricate details of costume such as lace trimmings, headdresses and gloves, and provide a fascinating insight into the dress of the mid-17th century.

As the 17th century progressed, costume and fashion continued to preoccupy engravers and increasing numbers of prints showing the dress of various sections of society were published, especially in France. Notable printmakers include Robert Boissard, who published a series of 24 engravings of fantastical costumes entitled *Mascarades* in 1597; Jean Dieu de St Jean (end of the 17th century) also sold designs of fashionable dress, engraved by F. Ertinger; and Sebastian

le Clerc also made engravings of French dress in the reign of Louis XIV.

Prints of fashionable dress were often probably produced to assist tailors and dressmakers in plying their trade and to help spread new fashions throughout Europe. Many followed a theme, showing figures in contemporary dress representing virtues, vices, fates or the seasons. Among the most prolific documenters of French costume at the close of the 17th century were the Bonnard family, Henri, Nicholas and Robert. They produced numerous prints showing the costumes of street traders, the Commedia dell'Arte, and the countries of Europe.

Few outstanding fashion subjects were published in the early decades of the 18th century, although one interesting exception was *The Exact Dress of the Head drawn from life at Court Opera Theatre from quality gentry of ye British Nation* published by Bernard Lens II in 1725–6. Around this time a flurry of illustrated books on dancing and deportment

appeared, such as L. P. Boitard's *The Rudiments of Genteel Behaviour*, published in 1737, with illustrations after B. Dandridge, detailing fashionable dress. Small-scale fashion illustrations were also produced in prolific quantities from the middle of the century for pocket books, small diaries, calendars and note books made for ladies to carry about with them.

In the 1770s, as fashion – both at court and amongst the public – became increasingly exaggerated, cartoonists began to publish illustrations highlighting its most ludicrous excesses. Philip Dawe produced notable caricature prints of fashionable ladies and gentlemen dandies known as Macaronis, who took fashion to the ultimate extreme with their enormous novelty wigs, high-heeled shoes, striped stockings, waistcoats and elaborate cravats. In France the growing obsession with fashionable dress also led to the publication of the first magazines entirely devoted to fashion plates. Some of the best

▲ La Revue de la Mode
Page from a 19th-century French magazine illustrated with coloured wood engravings, published by Abe Goubaud. Under **£5**

"You dropped this here Thingumbob Marm – Oh Dear, it's my bustle" One of many satirical fashion prints published in the early 19th century. **£40–50**

▶ Decorative prints
These gentlemen's fashion plates have been cut out, laid on modern paper and framed. Their value is therefore purely based on decorative appeal rather than the prints themselves.
£50–75

fashion plates were made in France. One of the earliest publications to include fashion plates was the *Galerie des Modes et des Costumes Français* (1778–87).

Over the following decades numerous other publications devoted to fashion appeared on the market including *Magazine des Modes Nouvelles, Françaises et Anglaises* and *Le Beau Monde*. Many of these magazines were also sold in England and English publications of the day also republished French plates. In England no magazines entirely devoted to fashion appeared until the end of the century, although plates appeared from the 1770s in publications such as the *Gentleman's Magazine* (1731–1907) and the *Ladies' Magazine* (1770–1828), which published plates from the French magazine *La Galerie des Modes Nouvelles*.

In England and in France most early fashion plates were either engraved or, more rarely, produced in aquatint. Among the

leading fashion plate artists were W. Alexander and J. A. Atkinson, both of whom worked for Heideloff's *Gallery of Fashion*. Expensive versions were sold with original hand-colouring. Many fashion plates which were originally sold uncoloured have been embellished at a later date and these are generally less desirable to today's collectors.

The *Gallery of Fashion* (1794–1803) was the earliest English publication entirely devoted to fashion. It contained illustrations by Nicholas van Heideloff, a talented engraver from Stuttgart who worked in Paris before coming to England to escape the French Revolution. The *Gallery of Fashion* appeared in monthly editions with two plates in each edition. Each plate typically included two or three figures and prints were hand-coloured aquatints with details painted in metallic gold and silver paint. This was, not surprisingly, an extremely expensive publication at the time and was sold by subscription for 3 guineas a year. After

▼ **Henri Lecomte Muletier**
Lithograph published 1818
from *Des Environs de
Burgos*, probably taken from
a folio of similar studies of
costumes. **£20–40**

◄ ▲ *Costume de Divers Pays*
Hand-coloured etchings
published in 1827 by Gatine
& La Mésangère.
£20–25 each

1800 the quality of the images declined and
many plates only contained single figures.
When the magazine ceased publication in
1803 a total of 217 plates had been published
and these are among the most highly sought-
after fashion plates today. Heideloff also
produced high-quality fashion illustrations
for Rudolph Ackermann's publication
Repository of the Arts.

In the late 18th and early 19th centuries,
as travel improved, there was a growing
demand for prints of national costumes, and
publications detailing dress in countries such
as China, Turkey and Russia as well as
Europe were increasingly popular both
in England and Europe. Many European
costume prints were probably bought as tourist
souvenirs along with topographical scenes,
which were also flourishing at this time.

National costumes of foreign countries
were often depicted in stipple engraving,
although some were made in aquatint.

During the 19th century improved printing
techniques, the development of lithography
and mechanization of printing processes, as
well as the growing demand for magazines
illustrating new fashions, gave rise to
increasing numbers of fashion publications.
The illustrations that appeared from the
mid-century onwards were of variable
quality with colours on cheaper publications
dictated more by what was available to the
printer rather than truly reflecting what
was fashionable. Nevertheless these plates
are often fascinating for the wealth of
terminology and detail they contain.

Among a plethora of publications that
appeared at this time were *La Belle Assemblée*
(1806–69), published both as a hand-coloured
version or in black and white; Townsend's
Selection of Parisian Costumes (1823–88); *The
Ladies' Cabinet* (1832–70); and *The English
Woman's Domestic Magazine* (1852–77), which
included plates by the French illustrator

▼ **Rudolf Ackermann**
Page from the famous publisher showing carnival and other picturesque costumes, probably intended to be pasted into albums. Sold unframed with a collection of other prints £100–200.

▶ **Military costumes**
19th-century lithograph from a series depicting German military dress, published in Berlin. £5–15

CARNIVAL COSTUMES. N7.

Published 1828 by R.ACKERMAN, 96 Strand, London.

▶ **After R. Bonnard**
Femme de Qualité à la Promenade
French late 18th-century engraving showing fashionably dressed ladies and their attendants. £70–90

David Jules, made originally for the French magazine *Le Moniteur de la Mode*.

Other outstanding late 19th-century designers of fashion plates include Anaïs and Isabella Toudouze. Anais designed plates for several publications including *La Mode Illustrée* and *Le Magazine des Demoiselles*, while her daughter Isabella designed plates for the Queen. The demand for fashion magazines spread to the United States; among the publications to appear were Graham's *American Monthly Magazine of Literature, Art and Fashion* and Godey's *Ladies' Book*.

With the advent of photography, the fashion plate declined in popularity and numbers of fashion plates gradually decreased. Few engravings and lithographs were produced after the 1920s but the fashions of this time gave rise to a final flowering of outstanding illustrations. Throughout the 1920s France continued to dominate the fashion scene with its illustrations of new styles of dress. Among the famous publications that employed some of the most accomplished artists were *La Gazette du Bon Ton*, *La Vie Parisienne* and *Vogue*.

One notable late exponent of the fashion plate was the leading Russian designer Raomain de Tirtoff – better known by the sobriquet Erté. Erté was famed for his magazine covers and original prints and was one of several illustrators of the 1920s to produce *pochoir* fashion prints, a form of hand-stencilled print, made using gouache or watercolour applied through stencils, often onto preprinted lithographic or collotype designs. The images produced were of far higher quality than mechanically made prints and some images were produced in smaller size for the magazine and as larger individual prints.

Georges Lepape was another leading fashion illustrator of the 1920s, whose work featured in fashion magazines in France and America as well as posters and books. Lepape's

▲▶ Victorian Fashion Plates
A pair of coloured etchings published 1866 as illustrations in *The English Woman's Domestic Magazine*, one of the popular 19th-century publications to include French fashion plates. Each under **£5**

illustrations encapsulate the new style of fashion illustration and include a series commissioned by the designer Paul Poiret, costume designs for Maeterlinck's *L'Oiseau Bleu* (1927), and cover designs for magazines such as *Vogue*, which invariably showed fashionably dressed ladies against a defiantly modern backdrop of skyscrapers. Other fashion illustrators of the early 20th century include Jean Dupas; Georges Barbier, whose work was reproduced as woodcuts, and André Marty. Many of the loose plates and illustrations made at this time in the Art Deco style were unsigned or by little-known artists and these are available today for very modest sums. Complete issues of the magazines of the 1920s are rare, however, and often command high prices. At auction fashion plates of the 1920s are often sold in sales devoted to the decorative arts of the period, while earlier plates often appear in costume and textile sales rather than general print sales.

Fashion plates are often highly decorative and keenly collected today, and although early examples are increasingly rare and much sought after, examples from the 19th century are still widely available for modest sums. Fashion plates enjoyed a great popularity in the late 18th and 19th centuries, when improved printing techniques allowed printmakers to produce details of costume and dress relatively inexpensively. The vast majority of fashion plates that appear individually framed in dealers' galleries today were originally published in one of the many fashion journals of the time, and on many images the name of the publication appears on the print line. High-quality, early examples from publications such as the *Gallery of Fashion* with original colouring are among the most sought after of fashion prints. Those with later colouring are far less desirable.

Modern Original Prints

Collecting 20th-century artists: from Picasso to contemporary printmakers

Many internationally renowned artists of the 20th century whose pioneering work helped shape the development of modern art also produced original prints. For these artists printmaking offered an alternative outlet for their artistic expression, allowing them to achieve effects not possible with other media.

Since the 1960s the term "original print" has been used in order to help avoid confusion and distinguish between mechanically produced reproductions and prints in which the artists themselves were intrinsically involved. In this sense the term "original print" is nowadays generally used to describe works that were developed and designed by the artist themselves as a print. In many cases artists became deeply involved in the technical processes required for the making of their prints although many also had expert assistance in the printmaking studio.

Original prints were made in limited editions, and from the early years of the 20th century were usually signed and numbered in the margin by hand in pencil. When the edition was complete the stones or plates were destroyed, and in the case of leading artists *catalogues raisonnés* of their work list the full details of any given work. If not numbered, certain impressions may instead be inscribed with letters. Among those commonly seen are AP – artist's proof – extra impressions of a print made for the artist's reference and friends; PP – printer's proof – another impression made for the printer's archive; HC – *hors de commerce* – prints made as samples not for sale; BAT – *bon à tirer* – approved and ready for final printing. The number of extra impressions varies but is usually listed in *catalogues raisonnés* of well-known artists. In general, artist's proofs constitute no more than 10 per cent of an edition. Value is not adversely affected if a print is a proof, and in certain cases they can be more desirable.

It is possible to buy original prints by even the best-known School of Paris artists very affordably. This is because in France there has been a long tradition of *livres d'artistes*, volumes which leading artists illustrated with original prints. These books were made on high-quality paper (usually Arches) unbound, with the illustrations interspersed with poetry.

◄ Elisabeth Frink
The Manciple's Tale, etching
with aquatint, published by
Leslie Waddington Prints in 1972
from *The Canterbury Tales*, signed,
inscribed and numbered. **£350–450**

► Henri Matisse
Original lithograph printed in sanguine in
1946 from an album, entitled *Visages* and
printed in an edition of 250. This linear
composition is typical of Matisse's style.
£600–900

◄ John Piper
Creysse, Dordogne, a screenprint
published in 1968, in an edition of
70, one of Piper's rarer and more
valuable subjects. **£2,000–3,000**

The illustrations were unsigned but each volume was signed by hand by the artist on the final sheet.

Another type of unsigned original print is that produced in the studios of Mourlot Frères, one of the main lithographic studios in Paris. When artists such as Chagall, Miró and Picasso made a signed lithograph in the studio (usually on Arches paper with wide margins), a further larger edition was produced from the same stones on cheaper wove paper with narrow margins. These were made in exactly the same way as signed prints, are listed in *catalogues raisonnés* and regarded as original prints – but because they are unsigned they are available for a fraction of the cost of signed works. Although unsigned works are less sought after on the international market and collectors buying for investment purposes may prefer to buy works with a signature, for collectors on a limited budget these offer a marvellous opportunity to buy high-quality yet affordable works by leading names.

Numerous different techniques are used to create prints: among the most popular methods are etching, lithography and screen printing. Many artists use several methods depending on the effect they wish to create although some specialize in one particular method. As a rule, images with colour tend to be more decorative and therefore more expensive than monochrome compositions. However, this is not always the case, since etchings are usually made in smaller editions than lithographs and a rare, interesting, black and white etching may be more valuable than a colourful lithograph made in a large edition. For the same reason monotypes are the rarest of original prints and command a premium.

Occasional fakes do appear on the market, and novice collectors can avoid these potentially costly pitfalls by always buying from a reputable source that guarantees the authenticity of the print. Original prints by major artists, whether signed or unsigned, are invariably well documented in *catalogues raisonnés* and dealers should be able to supply relevant information as a matter of course. It is important when checking prints against the catalogue to ensure that not only the image, but also the type of paper and the size should exactly match the catalogue description.

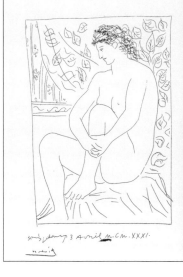

▲ **Marc Chagall**
Self-portrait,1960, published in *Les LIthographies de Chagall*. There was also a signed edition of this image which would be far more valuable. **£350–450**

◄ **Pablo Picasso**
Carmen, drypoint etching, 1949 from an edition of 320. Because this is unsigned it is far more modestly priced. **£600–900**

Europe

Among the most prolific of 20th-century print-makers was the Russian artist Marc Chagall, who worked in Paris, Germany and the United States and is regarded as one of the leading artists of the School of Paris. Though he produced etchings, some with aquatint or hand colouring, most of his prints were lithographs. His earlier work was mostly in black and white; the main body of his colour prints dates from after his exile to the United States during World War II. Chagall specialized in dreamlike scenes featuring lovers, biblical themes, bouquets of flowers and the circus, all of which proved highly popular when they were made. Although they can be slightly formulaic, they remain keenly sought after today. Like many print-makers, Chagall produced prints for book illustrations, some of which were separately published in folio editions, as well as single prints.

In common with many other leading artists of the day, Chagall produced prints both individually and in major series. Signed prints are extremely sought after and often highly priced and even unsigned editions of popular series are very desirable. More affordable prints are those published specially for inclusion in volume I of the *catalogue raisonné* of Chagall's lithographs published by

André Seuret in 1960; these are unsigned and were published in large editions on wove paper. Signed editions of the same series printed on Arches paper with margins were also made and are very highly priced although, as so often with Chagall, the main difference between the two editions is the signature.

Pablo Picasso was, similarly, a prolific maker of prints and is notable for the huge variety of techniques with which he experimented, including aquatint, etching, drypoint, lino cut and lithography. As with Chagall, his impressive *oeuvre* of original prints provides collectors with a rich hunting ground at a wide range of prices. Top examples of Picasso's coloured lithographs and lino cuts can fetch substantial sums but prints from larger editions and certain black and white etchings are among his less expensive works. Picasso produced prints as illustrations for *livres d'artistes* (see p84) and as major series, as well as single prints. As a general rule, earlier works tend to be more valuable than later ones, and, as with any work of art, the visual appeal of the subject matter also affects price.

Picasso's first attempt at printmaking came in 1905 when he produced *Les Saltimbanques*, a fascinating series of 15 drypoints and etchings based on his studies of a harlequin family. The series was first

◀ **Henri Matisse**
Martiniquaise, etching (1946) signed
in pencil numbered 1/25, on annam
appliqué paper. **£3,750–5,000**

◀ **Henri Matisse**
Mermaid, lithograph printed in sanguine
on Arches paper, from an album entitled
Florilège des Amours de Ronsard published
1948, in an edition of 320. The album was
signed on the back page. **£600–800**

▲ **Joan Miró**
Sculptures, a lithograph
printed in 1974, from an
edition of approximately
1,000, signed in the stone.
£500–700

published in 1913 by Vollard in an edition of only about 27 on *vieux japon* (japan paper), and in a larger edition of 250 on Van Gelder Zonen wove paper. Examples of the first edition are extremely rare, but those from the larger edition appear from time to time priced more modestly. Another sought-after early series in Picasso's neoclassical (also known as Ingres) style was the *Vollard Suite*, executed during the 1930s. Etchings and drypoints from this series are each signed and printed in editions of 300.

Another famous sequence of Picasso prints is the 347 series; a suite of 347 etchings and aquatints executed over a continuous period of seven months in 1968; each image is signed and was published in editions of 50. Many of these images are small-scale and prices are generally lower than for the *Vollard Suite*.

Illustrations from the *livre d'artiste Carmen* – by Prosper Merimée, published in 1949, are also good value. Picasso used the pure line of drypoint etching to depict Carmen's face in both the Cubist and classical styles. Carmen contains 35 etchings, each printed in editions of 320 on good-quality Montval wove paper and only available unsigned.

Henri Matisse was a far less prolific printmaker than either Picasso or Chagall, and original prints by him are relatively scarce by comparison.

Surprisingly for an artist regarded as one of the great colourists of the 20th century, most of his prints are monochrome. Matisse's printing methods included etching, lithography and stencil printing – a method of applying colour through cut stencils, known in France as *pochoirs*. Many of his prints rely on pure line to create volume, texture and space. Most of his subjects are figurative and among his most highly acclaimed work is a series of etched illustrations for Stéphane Mallarmé's *Poésies* (1932). Matisse also used lithography as an extension of drawing. Among his least expensive prints are faces drawn for a series of lithographs entitled *Visages* published in 1946 in an edition of 250. Printed in sanguine, these have the spontaneity of chalk drawings. Costlier Matisse prints include signed etchings, which were published in smaller editions, sometimes of no more than 25, and lithographs of more complex subjects such as nudes in interiors.

Many other leading European artists of the 20th century were also keen printmakers. The work of Joan Miró is particularly widely available on the market today, and other artists who also produced prints include Marino Marini, Bernard Buffet, Alberto Giacometti, Georges Braque, Wassily Kandinsky and Jean Arp.

► **David Hockney**
French Shop, etching
published in 1971,
signed and numbered in
pencil from an edition of
500. **£1,000–1,500**

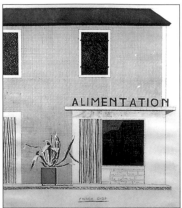

▼ **John Piper**
Walsoken, Norfolk, screenprint
published 1985, signed and
numbered from an edition of 70;
one of Piper's popular church
subjects. **£1,200–1,400**

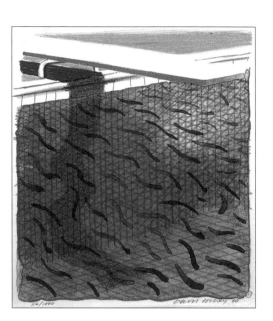

▲ **David Hockney**
*Pool made with paper and
blue ink for a book*, lithograph
signed and dated 1980 from an
edition of 1000, published with the
book *Paper Pools*. **£2,000–3,000**

Britain & the United States

Compared with the output of their European counterparts, works by leading British artists are generally less expensive because, with a few exceptions, their reputations are not so well established on the international market. Among the leading British contemporary printmakers are John Piper, David Hockney, Elisabeth Frink, Henry Moore and Howard Hodgkin.

One of the few British artists to establish themselves on the international market, David Hockney is also one of the most prolific British printmakers of the 20th century. Prices for Hockney's work peaked in the 1980s and, in common with most other collecting areas, fell at the end of the decade. Recent years have seen values steadying.

Hockney's early work was mainly in black and white and he is regarded as one of the leading etchers of the 1960s and 1970s – the subtlety and

accomplishment of his etching technique has been compared to that of 18th-century engravers. The subject matter of Hockney's printed work is, however, far from traditional. It is typically inspired by the accoutrements of contemporary life: Hockney specializes in dispassionately observed scenes of swimming pools, restaurants, cars and skyscrapers, often populated by fashionably dressed figures. His most famous early prints were made as book illustrations, such as *Illustrations for Thirteen Poems by C. P. Cavafy*, published in 1966 by Editions Alecto in an edition of 75. Another highly acclaimed series is *Illustrations for Six Fairy Tales from the Brothers Grimm*, published in 1969.

Hockney was a passionate admirer of Picasso's work and used techniques developed by Aldo Crommelynk, Picasso's printmaker, to etch in colour one of his most famous folios, *The Blue*

▶ **Elizabeth Blackadder**
Still life with Lily and Flute, etching in six colours with goldleaf, published 1991, from an edition of 200. **£400–500**

▲ **Henry Moore**
Mother and child 8, etching published in 1983 on Arches paper, signed in pencil and numbered from a full edition of 75.
£900–1,200

▶ **Henry Moore**
Mother and Child, lithograph published in 1967, signed and numbered. An edition of 255 from a series of seven prints made for Moore's *Shelter Sketchbook*.
£1,200–1,800

Guitar, a series of 20 etchings, published 1976–77, based on a poem by Wallace Stevens, that was itself inspired by Picasso. A series of prints of swimming pools published in 1980 are also among Hockney's most famous; the single print entitled *Pool made with paper and blue ink for a book* was issued in a large edition of 1,000 and is among his most loved and affordable works. Many of Hockney's colour lithographs were produced on a large scale and prices for these can rise to substantial sums. Hockney also experimented with homemade prints produced on an office photocopier, which he signed and numbered in the usual way. These are also keenly sought after by collectors.

Another prolific British artist who has enjoyed huge popularity as a printmaker is John Piper. Piper is best known for his prints of architectural subjects and churches, and rose to fame during World War II for his architectural compositions which recorded the effects of bomb damage on the English landscape. Piper used many different media including etching, screen printing and lithography and his prints have risen considerably in popularity and price in recent years particularly when they have churches and colourful architectural subjects.

During the 1950s prints became increasingly popular and a new generation of artists and sculptors also began to create prints using various techniques including etching, lithography and aquatint. Henry Moore, although best known as a sculptor, also became a prolific printmaker at this time and his figurative and semi-abstract subjects invariably reflect his interest in three-dimensional form. Moore's work is rarely coloured and his simpler figurative compositions and animal subjects are among his most popular works. Most of his works

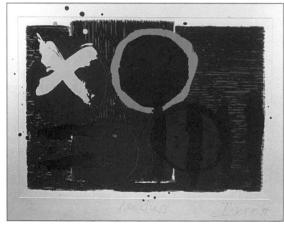

◄ Bruce McLean
Another night out on Sausage Street, a screenprint published 1996, signed in pencil from an edition of 250. **£250–350**

▼ Elisabeth Frink
Green Man, a grey screenprint published 1992, signed and numbered from an edition of 70, published by Curwen Chilford, the last set of prints made by the artist before her death. **£1,100–1,400**

◄ Albert Irvin
New Cross, screen and woodblock print published in 1994 signed and numbered in pencil from an edition of 225. **£300–400**

were signed both in the stone and in pencil, and for an artist of international status, his work remains good value. Editions are usually small; a typical Moore print is *Eight Reclining Figures*, an original lithograph published 1966, in a signed edition of 75 on japon nacré paper.

Another important sculptor also known for her powerful prints is Elisabeth Frink. Like Moore's her images strongly reflect her interest in sculptural forms. Much of Frink's work has risen in price in recent years although certain subjects remain more valuable than others: images of horses and dogs are particularly sought after and heads are also popular, while prints from her series illustrating *The Canterbury Tales* are more modestly priced.

Abstract artists also turned their hand to print-making and among the most esteemed is the artist Howard Hodgkin. Some of Hodgkin's best prints

have been produced in the last decade and their value depends greatly on the richness and vibrancy of the colouring. Earlier screen prints and lithographs with a flatter, less characteristic appearance are less sought after. Etchings produced with hand colouring are often his best works, and are highly collectable.

Other well-known British artist-printmakers of recent decades whose work remains popular are Peter Blake and Richard Hamilton. Their work, like that of Hockney, reflects the influence of Pop Art. Abstraction has been explored in compelling prints by William Scott and Victor Pasmore. Edward Bawden is best known for his architectural prints in which pattern and design play a strong part; and Stanley William Hayter worked in Paris and the United States experimenting with different printmaking methods to produce abstract images of striking originality.

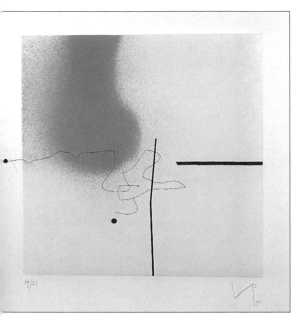

◄ **Victor Pasmore**
Magic Eye, a series of seven etchings with aquatint signed in pencil and numbered from an edition of 35. **£450–550**

◄ **Howard Hodgkin**
Red Eye, lithograph, published in 1981, signed in pencil and numbered from the edition of 100. **£800–900**

▲ **Jim Dine**
Rancho, woodcut printed in colours in 1982 on B. F. K. Reeves paper. Signed, dated and numbered 45/75 and published by Pace, New York. **£3,000–4,000**

Leading American artists of the later decades of the 20th century have also turned their hand to printmaking. Jasper Johns and Robert Rauschenberg, preeminent artists of the Abstract Expressionist movement, produced heavily coloured lithographs that promoted their ideas. Similarly the American Pop Art movement spawned several influential printmakers who rebelled against the established aesthetic precepts, embracing commercial, mechanical and photographic techniques, while concentrating on deliberately contemporary subject matter – soup tins, comic strips and film stars. Among the leading Pop Art printmakers were Andy Warhol and Roy Lichtenstein. Both exploited new mechanical printing processes using offset lithography and photographic techniques in their screen printing. Warhol is perhaps best known for his iconic silkscreen images of Marilyn Monroe printed using a stencil silkscreen and an enlarged photographic image. Warhol made numerous silkscreens using this method, of which signed versions are most collectable. Warhol made numerous reprints of his most popular images and value can therefore vary depending on the edition from which a print is taken and on whether or not it is signed.

Another accomplished American printmaker, Jim Dine, is best known for his expressionist etchings which are heavily worked with scraping and scratching out to extraordinarily evocative effect. Dine often combines etching with hand colouring and monotype and his most desirable work from small signed and numbered editions is highly sought after. Dine also produced interesting woodcuts, some printed in monochrome black and white or grey, black and white, and these tend to be slightly less valuable.

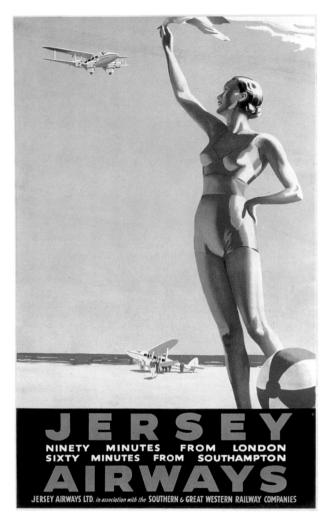

◄ **Collectable posters**
Colourful posters advertising air travel, such as this anonymous example for Jersey Airways, are very collectable. **£600–800**

Posters

The colourful advertising poster that has become so much a part of everyday life has a relatively short history. It was only at the end of the 19th century, when developments in lithographic printing enabled colour images to be mass-produced cheaply, that the poster as we know it first began to appear. Since then advertising posters have become ubiquitous. In France, where the poster first flourished, the public was quick to realize their artistic significance, even going so far as to cut them down under cover of darkness when they were first posted. Elsewhere the poster enjoyed mixed fortunes; many were disposed of in huge quantities as new images were printed to take their place and it is only more recently that posters have become increasingly collectable.

What & how to collect
For today's collectors the appeal of posters lies largely in the reason they were successful in the first place –

their immediate visual impact. Most collectors tend to specialize in posters of a certain type and some of the most popular collecting areas are dealt with on the following pages. Flick through an auction catalogue and you will come across posters advertising transport of all types, exotic locations, picturesque scenery, sporting events, food and drink and theatrical personalities – all appealing subjects that could form the theme for a collection. Alternatively you could concentrate on the work of a particular artist, or artists of a certain nationality, or focus on posters of a particular style, such as Art Nouveau or Art Deco.

There are now specialist poster dealers, some of whom exhibit at antiques fairs; sales devoted entirely to the subject are held in some major auction houses each year, as well as poster sections in some print sales. Posters for recent films and promoting pop events are generally included in specialist auctions of rock and pop or entertainment memorabilia.

Learning about posters
The growing interest in posters has given rise to a large number of specialist books covering in detail many of their main themes such as railways, motoring and winter sports, as well as *catalogues raisonnés* of posters by certain artists. There are also numerous archives and museums containing general and specialist collections of posters (see p155).

Anyone beginning a collection should also spend as much time as possible visiting auction houses and dealers to examine posters closely. However many books you read, there is no substitute for "hands-on" experience; handling the genuine article is by far the best way of learning to spot reproductions and fakes.

Auction house catalogues are also filled with useful information about the posters on offer. Most zwill state the name of the artist, if known, the title of the poster, the printing technique – usually lithography, the date of printing, the size and a price guide. The price guide given in a catalogue entry should not however be taken as a cast iron guarantee that a poster will sell between the limits. Auctioneers, however experienced, can never predict with certainty how badly two collectors might want a particularly desirable poster. Many auction catalogues also give details of the condition of the poster and note whether the poster is framed or backed on linen. Bear in mind that the price guide does not include commission or VAT on the commission which is added to the hammer price, and that you should always examine anything you buy very closely to satisfy yourself as to its condition. If a poster is in very poor condition you also need to take into account the cost of having it professionally restored, cleaned and mounted.

Authenticity & fakes

Fakes are generally few and far between although there are three problem areas of which new collectors should be wary: first, and most commonly, reprints of genuine works by known poster artists; second, fake works bearing the spurious signature of a well-known artist; and finally, posters which are pastiches of sought-after styles, such as Art Deco, sometimes signed with an unknown artist's name. Most "fakes" are of images by the most valuable artists such as Toulouse-Lautrec whose work has been much reprinted since the beginning of this century. However, all Toulouse-Lautrec's posters are well documented and provided collectors buy from a reputable source that guarantees the authenticity of the poster, they should have little to worry about.

Posters with fake Cassandre signatures include a spurious poster for *Croix Verte*. Among the few other fake posters that have appeared on the market in recent years is a poster in the Art Deco style, signed by Maurice Dufrène for *Rayon des Soieries*, and a poster for *Lord* signed Garretto bearing the name of a Milanese printer. Some posters by Mucha have been extensively reprinted; however, these are usually identifiable by the fact that the paper is of superior quality and much whiter than that used on originals.

Most reproductions are made using photographic offset lithographic techniques. These are often identifiable by the fact that the image is made up of a series of tiny dots, visible through a magnifying glass. Size and the name of the printer can also be a giveaway of a later reprint – posters were printed in standard sizes (listed on p150) that are often different from those of reproductions, and certain artists are associated with certain printers. For example Chéret was published by Chaix; Champenois usually published Mucha; Serre usually published Broders; P. Vercasson usually published Cappiello, and Swiss posters were often printed by Wolfenburger (or Wolfsberg), Wasserman or Fretz.

Value

For most posters the key factors that affect value are similar to those governing most other forms of art. The reputation of the artist is of primary importance. By far the most expensive posters are those by Toulouse-Lautrec, since their value is boosted by his reputation as an international artist. Posters by other leading names or artistic groups such as Alphonse Mucha, the Viennese Secessionists and rare Russian

Constructivist posters can also fetch very high prices. Value is also enormously affected by rarity. All posters are multiples and most were originally printed in considerable numbers; therefore examples by important artists that are in limited supply are more desirable than those which are abundantly available.

Since posters were produced in quantity, and there is rarely a reliable way of knowing how many have survived, "rarity" can fluctuate with dramatic effect on prices. In the case of the Russian Constructivists, works were very rare and commanded huge sums until the collapse of the Soviet Union brought about a relaxation of tight export controls and allowed more posters to appear on the Western market. The result was a fall in prices. Similarly, Roger Broders' work was scarce and prices rose steeply until a large collection of his travel posters recently appeared on the market. Although prices did not fall, the increase prices steadied, and only now are they climbing slowly again.

Design

Although many posters are signed in the design and works by certain artists are keenly collected, there is also a wealth of posters by lesser artists and numerous unsigned examples. The value of these is largely dependent on the quality of the design and commercial appeal of the image. Good design will invariably hold its value, even if the poster is by an obscure or anonymous artist. Also popular are posters showing sports, vintage cars and fashionable figures, or those that reflect the mood of their times.

Condition

Condition is of great importance in valuing posters. Most (apart from Swiss posters) were printed on inexpensive paper because they were not intended to last, and as a result will have suffered some wear. Many of the posters sold at auction are in need of restoration and the damage is clearly visible. If you buy from dealers the poster may have already been restored, but you should still find out what exactly has been done. While small creases and tears are acceptable posters, with serious damage are best avoided. Posters that have been extensively restored are usually not desirable unless they are particularly rare. Finally, never be afraid to seek the advice of experts, who are usually happy to share their experience. Most will probably tell you that provided you buy from a reputable source and collect only posters that genuinely appeal to you, rather than as an investment, your collection will give you great lasting pleasure – and any increase in value will be an extra bonus when you decide to sell.

Art Nouveau Posters

The evolution of early posters and the development of Art Nouveau throughout Europe

The early history of posters parallels both the rise of the Art Nouveau movement and advances in printing techniques. During the closing decades of the 19th century, until the advent of World War I, a dynamic new decorative style spread through Europe, dramatically changing the face of the applied and pictorial arts. The movement is generally thought to have taken its name from the Parisian gallery Maison de l'Art Nouveau where objects in the new style were exhibited.

Numerous influences played a part in the evolution of Art Nouveau. The style reflects the impact of the influx of works of art from Japan that began to filter through to Europe after the end of Japan's economic isolation from the Western world for nearly 200 years. Organic forms, surface pattern and strong use of colour were elements derived from oriental works of art and, in particular, Japanese woodblocks that became a distinctive feature of the Art Nouveau style. In England the style's origins were associated with the interest in traditional designs and medieval art that preoccupied the Arts and Crafts movement pioneered by William Morris. Its development was also inextricably linked to Liberty, the London shop, where many leading Art Nouveau designers sold their wares.

Throughout Europe designers interpreted Art Nouveau in various ways. Designers in Spain formed the Catalan movement; in Switzerland and Italy the style, known as "Liberty style", permeated the work of designers such as Carlo Bugatti; the French referred to Art Nouveau as *le style anglais*; while in Germany it was known as *Jugendstil* and in Austria as the Secessionist movement.

Alongside the evolution of Art Nouveau, the development of lithography (see pp38–9), together with the economic prosperity and political stability of the late 19th century and a rapidly increasing population, created a ready demand for advertising. Prior to the use of lithography, posters had been used to advertise events such as theatrical productions using the letter press, wood block printing

technique. These were generally small, dominated by typography, chromatically limited and of little visual interest. As the potential of lithography was developed, manufacturers in Paris discovered that posters of larger size and greater colour variation could be commercially viable and provide them with an effective method of advertising their products. Theatres, which had traditionally used posters to advertise their programmes, were among the first to make use of the new poster, but soon posters were used to advertise a wide range of consumer products from food to fashion to travel.

France led the field in the development of posters, and during the 1870s pictorial images became larger and more important in the overall design. By the 1880s, visually arresting posters became so ubiquitous that a law was passed to restrict their use and the consequent defacing of buildings.

Even from the earliest days in France, posters were admired and avidly collected as works of art. Widespread French interest in

posters gave rise to magazines such as *Les Maîtres de l'Affiche*, *L'Estampe Moderne* and *La Plume* which published popular posters in A4 and A3 format. In Paris, poster artists also held exhibitions of their work at galleries such as the Salon des Cents. Some of the leading designers of the period were artists in their own right; others worked purely as commercial artists. By far the most sought-after and valuable posters are those by Toulouse-Lautrec, who produced only 31 poster designs, and whose value is largely based on his reputation as a leading artist. Among the other most sought-after designers of posters in the Art Nouveau style Alphonse Mucha, Jules Chéret and Privat Livemont also have international reputations. The enduring popularity of Art Nouveau images has given rise to numerous reprints and reproductions. Some of these date from the early decades of the 20th century and can be very difficult for inexperienced collectors to identify, and it is important therefore to buy from a reputable source, or to take expert advice if in doubt.

◀ Jules Chéret
This poster was printed
c.1893 to advertise a
fashionable drink,
Cacao Lhara.
£1,000–1,200

▶ Jules Chéret
The use of brilliant colour
and a seductive female
figure, as seen here in
Olympia, are hallmarks of
most of Chéret's posters.
£1,000–1,500

Henri de Toulouse-Lautrec
A poster promoting a fashionab
turn of the century Parisian theatr
Le Divan Japonais, the design show
Yvette Gilbert, a famous theatric
star on the stage. **£10,000–15,00**

◀ Henri de Toulouse-Lautrec
Published in 1896, this poster
advertised the *Elles* series of
lithographs, which depicted life in
Parisian brothels. **£4,000–5,000**

French Art Nouveau

Generally regarded as the grandfather of the poster, Jules Chéret was a French-born commercial artist who achieved a huge output and one of the first designers to exploit the artistic potential of the poster. Chéret began producing lithographic posters in the late 1850s after a visit to England where he had come into contact with new printing machinery invented by Senefelder for mass-producing colour lithographs. On his return to Paris Chéret set up his own press, the *Imprimerie Chaix*, in 1866 where he perfected the art of designing and publishing his colourful, lively designs.

Chéret was an extremely prolific designer; the *catalogue raisonné* of his work lists 1,069 different designs and these were often printed in vast quantities. Chéret's designs parallel the development of the poster. Early examples are dominated by lettering and rather fussy in overall effect. As the 19th century progressed his posters became increasingly striking and simple with less lettering. Nearly all Chéret's

designs feature an attractive lady in a theatrical stance holding the product which forms the subject of the advertisement. In most designs shades of red, yellow and orange predominate, backgrounds are sketchily defined with black or grey, and designs are defined with strong black outline and little detail.

Chéret designed posters for a huge range of subjects, and often made several different designs for the same product; for example he created 13 different posters for Saxoléine, a variety of lamp paraffin. Theatrical subjects include a poster for Loïe Fuller, a celebrated performer known for her titillating dance of veils.

Although early designs are rarer, collectors tend to prefer Chéret's later, more colourful designs. Value varies according to the visual appeal of the image and its rarity. Chéret's posters were produced in several standard sizes of which the most common are 93 x 32 in/236 x 83cm (two sheets); 47 x 32in/121 x 83cm (one sheet), and value can be affected by the

▲ **Jules Chéret**
Bal au Moulin Rouge,
printed by Chaix, the
sense of movement
and dynamism are
typical of Chéret.
£700–900

size. A poster entitled *Palais de Glace* was printed in both sizes and in good condition fetches ten times more for the larger size than the smaller version. Other popular subjects include *Théâtrophone* and *Benzo Moteur*. Chéret's work was immensely popular in its day, so much so that he was awarded the Légion d'honneur for bringing "art" to commercial printing. His designs were reprinted in his lifetime in *Les Maîtres de l'Affiche* and *L'Estampe Moderne*, and these are also collectable although less valuable than original posters.

Perhaps the most influential poster artist of the late 19th century was Toulouse-Lautrec, an aristocratic artist whose designs worked by dramatic and uncompromising honesty rather than the obvious decorative appeal that made Chéret so appealing. Lautrec's posters are heavily influenced by Japanese woodcuts and rely on flat areas of colour and strong use of black for their striking visual impact. His figures are often sketchy, spontaneous but almost grotesque in appearance, and the lettering plays little part in the design. Lautrec designed only 31 posters, the vast majority of which were for the theatre – among them are the most valuable posters ever printed. Most were published in editions of 3,000 and all have been the subject of exhaustive research; in many cases the models for the figures have been identified. Value depends greatly on rarity; the most expensive poster by Lautrec is *La Gitane* of which only two examples have come up in public auction. Lautrec's posters were always signed either with a monogram or full signature in the design and have been widely reprinted and reproduced. The quality of the paper is often the best way to tell if the poster is genuine. Among the most frequently faked Lautrec posters are *Le Divan Japonais* and *Jane Avril*. Reprints are often discernible only by slight variations in the print, and by the absence of overlapping colours which should be visible at the edges of the design.

▶ **Théophile
Alexandre Steinlen**
L'Assommoir, printed in 1900.
The poster advertises a new play
by Emile Zola. **£2,500–3,500**

▲ **Privat Livemont**
Biscuits de Beukelaer, printed in Brussels,
1900. The stylized vegetal background is
typical of Livemont's work. **£1,500–2,000**

International Art Nouveau

Numerous artists and designers flourished in Paris around the turn of the century, and many, like the Czech Alphonse Mucha, came from other parts of Europe to make their career in the French capital, which became the artistic and cultural centre of Europe. One of the earliest and most influential was the artist Pierre Bonnard whose posters *Salon des Cent*, *La Revue Blanche* and *France Champagne* influenced Toulouse-Lautrec.

Théophile Alexandre Steinlen was another outstanding early poster designer. The son of an artist, Steinlen was born and educated in Lausanne and came to Paris in 1881 where he found work as a designer of printed textiles and began producing posters soon after. Steinlen's posters often show scenes from the Parisian *demi-monde*, and he was also particularly fond of depicting cats and dogs. One of his best-known posters was for sterilized milk, entitled *Lait Pur Stérilisé*, and shows a child

sipping a bowl of milk while three cats look on. Leonetto Cappiello, an extremely prolific Italian artist working in Paris at this time, designed numerous food and drink posters as well as some for fashion accessories including corsets and hats. Cappiello's designs often show a single female figure against a solid background of colour. Shades of black, red, yellow and brown are reminiscent of Chéret although the figures are less sketchily drawn. Other leading designers include the Italian-born Manuel Orazi , who designed a famous poster for the department store La Maison Moderne; Jean de Paléologue, a Hungarian whose posters include designs for bicycles; Eugène Grasset, a Swiss-born architect; Lucien Faure and Jules Alexandre Grun.

In Belgium posters also began to be produced reflecting the fashionable Art Nouveau style. Perhaps the best known of the Belgian artists was Privat Livemont, whose work shows the impact of

◀ **Fernand Toussaint**
Ville de Bruxelles, printed in 1914, is an example of the numerous tourist posters produced in Belgium in the early decades of the century. **£600–800**

▶ **Leonetto Cappiello**
The strong flat colours and bold outlines of this poster for *Corset le Furet*, printed in 1901, reflect the influence of Japanese woodcuts. **£800–1,000**

Collecting
Alphonse Mucha

▲ **Alphonse Mucha**
Among Mucha's less expensive works are small menus, such as this commissioned by a brand of cognac, c.1897. **£500–800**

Mucha and Chéret in its use of stylized figures, floral and organic motifs and strong colour. Fernand Toussaint is another artist whose Belgian coastal views are popular, as are his rare designs depicting elegant women. Toussaint's images are typically livelier than those of Livemont. Other artists produced more colourful, less stylized images advertising the Belgian coast, including Van Acker, Florimond and François Dumont (see also pp118–19). Many examples are anonymous, but leading publishers in Brussels, where most were produced, included O. de Rycker & Mendel (who published Privat Livemont) and J. E. Goossens.

In Holland poster design lagged slightly behind the rest of Europe, although two leading designers to emerge in Amsterdam were J. G. van Caspel and Willy Sluiter. Caspel designed posters for a wide range of products including bicycles, soap, foods, photographic materials and even life insurance.

One of the most famous artists whose posters have become synonymous with Art Nouveau is Alphonse Mucha. A Czech artist born in Prague, he trained in stage design in Vienna before rising to prominence as the designer of posters for the leading actress Sarah Bernhardt. Mucha's designs are highly detailed, and invariably feature a scantily clad or naked female figure with long elaborately coiffed hair. The subject is often framed within a decorative border and frequently breaks though the frame in parts of the design. Backgrounds frequently contain stylized floral decoration and often the main subject and the additional decoration have sensuous, sexual overtones.

Mucha made many of his designs in series of four – the four seasons, four hours, four jewels – and the value of a complete set is considerably greater than for a single piece from a set that has been broken up. Some of his works were, unusually, of small dimension and used as menus and calendars, and today these are among his more affordable works. Colouring was subtle; shades of green, blue and brown are typical and the quality of the colour is important in establishing value. Mucha was particularly fond of gilding, which can be prone to wear. Designs are usually signed in the block.

► **Alejandro de Riquer**
Poster advertising *Granja Avicola de Sn. Luis*. De Riquer was one of Spain's most prolific Art Nouveau poster designers. £300–500

▼ **Edward Penfield**
Harper's March, 1896. Penfield made a series of posters for Harper's. His use of solid blocks of colour reflects the influence of Toulouse-Lautrec. £250–350

Jugendstil, the German name for the Art Nouveau style, also inspired designers in Berlin and Munich where the poster industry was centred. Publishing provided designers with some of the most interesting early commissions.

One of the leading publications in Berlin was the magazine *Pan* founded by Julius Meier Graefe and Otto Bierbaum. The magazine commissioned advertising posters in the Art Nouveau style both by native and leading international artists. Toulouse-Lautrec was commissioned to produce a poster for the magazine in 1895 but German taste was far more rigid than that of Paris and Toulouse-Lautrec's design, decried as ugly and revealing, caused an uproar, leading to the dismissal of the editor. Several other publications were also important patrons of poster designers including *Simplicissimus*, *Die Jugend*, *Deutsche Kunst und Dekoration* and *Sturm*, and German designers also produced posters for theatres and exhibitions and a range of consumer products. Among the leading German designers

were Ludwig Hohlwein and Thomas Theodor Heine, whose angular, crudely drawn poster for *Simplicissimus* featuring a snarling bulldog presages the violent images of Expressionism.

Although Italian posters do not survive in such vast quantities as those produced in France, Italy also fell under the spell of Art Nouveau and in the main centres of Milan and Turin, highly sophisticated posters characterized by their refined use of colour and elegant design were produced. In Milan the publisher G. Ricordi & Co. dominated poster production and employed several leading designers including Mataloni, Adolfo Hohenstein and Leopoldo Metlicovitz. Ricordi were also important publishers of music including opera scores and many of the posters they produced provided the advertising for these productions. Another of Ricordi's important clients was the Mele chain of stores and some strikingly detailed designs were produced for hats, clothes and other goods sold in their shops. Most Italian posters featured an

▲ **Ludwig Hohlwein**
Café de l'Odéon, printed 1908 in Munich. Hohlwein was one of Germany's leading poster designers. **£3,000–4,000**

◄ **Adolfo Hohenstein**
The elegant and sophisticated design of this poster dating from 1898 is typical of Italian Art Nouveau. **£3,000–5,000**

idealized female figure who is often semi-naked, and movement and dramatic colours are features of many of the best designs. Early Italian posters by leading designers are rare and highly sought after by collectors, both in Italy and the rest of Europe.

As with Belgian designs, posters made in Spain at this time reflect the influence of Art Nouveau tempered by naturalism. Spanish Art Nouveau centred on the city of Barcelona which enjoyed a period of great economic prosperity in the 1890s. Alejandro de Riquer created highly decorative detailed images which show the influences of Mucha's designs combined with a more realistic approach. De Riquer had travelled extensively throughout Europe and was also an accomplished landscape artist, book illustrator and designer of stained glass. His reputation as a poster designer was based on his posters advertising a variety of grain, *Granja Avicola de Sn. Luis*. One example (see above) shows a typical Art Nouveau female figure with bowed head mothering a clutch of chicks on her lap. De Riquer also

designed posters for shops, novels and exhibitions. Miquel Utrillo, again based in Barcelona, also produced stylish posters notable for their strong colours and dramatic design.

Art Nouveau posters were also produced in America where the leading exponents of the new stylish images include Maxfield Parrish, Edward Penfield and Will Bradley. American designers were heavily influenced by the work of European artists, particularly Aubrey Beardsley, William Morris, Toulouse-Lautrec and Mucha.

Penfield and Parrish were both well-known book illustrators who turned their hand to poster designing. Penfield was Art Director for *Harper's* magazine for whom he produced advertising posters. The example illustrated on the facing page reflects the influence both of Toulouse-Lautrec and of Japanese woodcuts. Penfield and other leading American designers are keenly collected in both Britain and the United States although their work is still affordable.

▲ **Ludwig Hohlwein**
An example of the influence of
Secessionism in Munich, this
poster was printed in 1908.
£500–800

◄ **Koloman Moser**
Ver Sacrum V Jahr XIII, an extremely
rare poster from 1903 made for one of
the Viennese Secessionist exhibitions,
designed by one of the movement's
founder members. **£50,000–60,000**

Secessionists

Towards the end of the 19th century in Germany
and Vienna an influential group of architects
and designers began a rebellion against what they
considered to be a decline in prevailing aesthetic
taste. Exhibiting their new style of art was difficult
to achieve through the usual established artistic
channels so they "seceded" forming avant-garde
associations in Munich in 1892, in Vienna in 1897
and in Berlin in 1899 to give voice to their new-
found beliefs. Of these three societies the *Wiener
Sezession* (Vienna Secession) was perhaps the most
influential in the development of poster design.
Members of the Vienna Secession included architects, artists and designers such as Otto Wagner,
Josef Maria Olbrich, Josef Hoffmann, Gustav
Klimt, Koloman Moser and Adolf Loos.
Architecture played a central role in the appearance
of all Secessionist art and their architectural ideals

revolved around their preoccupation with the rela-
tionship between form and function. In this they
were strongly influenced by similar artistic movements elsewhere in Europe, such as William Morris
and the Arts and Craft movement in England and
the streamlined designs of Charles Rennie
Mackintosh and the Glasgow School.

Although Secessionism was generally seen as an
adjunct of the European Art Nouveau movement,
the Secessionists went one step further in question-
ing the role of superfluous ornament and their
refined, streamlined designs in many ways bridge
the gap between the stylized forms of Art Nouveau
and the angular modernity of Art Deco.

Many members of the Viennese Secessionist
movement worked in a building called Ver Sacrum
(The Rite of Spring) where they exhibited their
work and produced a journal by the same name.

▼ **Franz von Stuck**
Munich art exhibition poster, 1905. German
posters reflecting the influence of Secessionism
are generally far less costly than Austrian
examples. £800–1,200

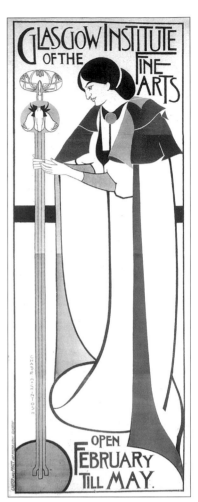

► **Charles Rennie Mackintosh**
Mackintosh's streamlined forms proved
influential in the development of Secessionist
design. This rare poster for the Glasgow
Institute of the Fine Arts would be worth
£40,000–60,000.

Ver Sacrum was published between 1898 and 1903 and its artistic manifestos were illustrated with examples of the work of its leading members. The Ver Sacrum building was designed by Olbrich, who also designed posters for exhibitions held there. Other leading poster designers were Gustav Klimt, Koloman Moser, Josef Hoffmann, Alfred Roller and Ferdinand Andri. Many of these designers were also involved in the *Wiener Werkstätte* (Viennese Workshops), founded by Hoffmann in 1903 to introduce purer forms into other areas of design including furniture, metalwork and glass.

Secessionist posters are often characterized by their highly stylized images and the importance of geometric pattern and balance in the overall design. Lettering is nearly always integral to the design and colours are often limited in range with black often heavily used. Unlike posters by French artists such as Chéret, Secessionist posters were printed in strictly limited numbers for an elite audience. For this reason they are very rare today, and prices for poor-quality Viennese examples start at £4,000 rising to £100,000 or more for a good example in good condition. Posters by Mackintosh and his followers in the Glasgow School are also highly priced, but slightly less so than those by their leading counterparts in Vienna. Of the Secessionists, works by Klimt are the most valuable and sought after; collectors should be aware that his posters have been reprinted and faked. Among the more affordable Secessionist posters are those printed in Munich by artists such as Stuck and Hohlwein. In general, Secessionist posters were printed on better-quality paper than those made in France. Printers' names, such as A. Berger and Gesellschaft für Graphische Industrie, are usually marked in the margin.

Russian Constructivism

Collecting the graphic art of Russia's leading avant-garde artists and designers

ЮБКИ ДЖОНА

В ГЛ. РОЛИ
ВИЛЬЯМ ХАРТ

▲ **Photomontage**
The use of close-up portraits and
photomontage are characteristic of
many designs. This poster by the
Stenberg brothers advertises the
1927 film *John's Skirts*. **£2,000–4,000**

One of the most important artistic movements of the early 20th century, Russian Constructivism evolved as a direct result of the Russian Revolution and enjoyed significant success during the 1920s and 1930s. The Constructivist movement was founded in Russia in 1917 by the sculptor Antoine Pevsner and his younger brother Naum Pevsner Gabo. The group espoused Utopian beliefs about art which they felt should be functional and non-elitist and incorporate newly available materials and technology. Ironically many of the champions of this idealistic movement were subsequently either forced into exile or imprisoned.

Although initially founded as a movement primarily concerned with sculpture, posters became an important aspect of the Constructivist's art, and designs are characterized by angular lines and abstract shapes. Colours are usually strictly limited with black, white and red the most predominant shades. Most are produced using mechanical printing techniques, with elements taken from photography and architecture. The film industry and contemporary theatre were important patrons of the new style but, whatever their subject matter, all Constructivist posters have a political undertone. In their modernity and use of modern typography and photomontage effects, many of the designs reflect their designer's interest in Cubism and other contemporary European artistic movements.

Leading Constructivist poster designers include the writer and thinker Alexander Rodchenko, Vladimir Mayakovskii, Kazimir

▼ **Vladimir & George Stenberg**
Poster for the film *The Shooting of Dan McGrew*, published 1927 in an edition of 15,000. The Stenberg brothers were among the most prolific designers of avant-garde Russian film posters during the 1920s, producing around 300 different images.
£1,500–2,500

◀ **Stenberg & Rukhlevsky**
This poster was designed by the Sternberg brothers and Yakov Rukhlevsky. It advertised the film *Decembrist*, which starred the leading actors Michurin and Lebedev. **£2,000–4,000**

Malevich and George and Vladimir Stenberg who developed photomontage posters and worked for the Russian film industry. Other artists associated with film posters include Anton Lavinski and Boris Prusakov whose poster for the film *Battleship Potemkin* is one of the most famous of Russian film posters.

One of the most famous posters of the period by El Lissitzky, entitled *Beat the Whites with the Red Wedge*, produced in 1919, represents the typical Constructivist poster: an overtly political subject; a composition made of simple shapes inspired by collage; and the red, white and black colour scheme. Many of El Lissitzky's posters also incorporate photographic elements inspired by contemporary films; a poster for the Russian Exhibition in Zurich in 1929 includes superimposed photographic portraits.

During the Cold War, Constructivist posters appeared rarely on the market and nothing came out of Russia legally. Following the collapse of the Soviet Union, material has come out in large quantities both legally and illegally. At first the market for this material boomed and prices rose, but as a result fakes began appearing and this undermined collector confidence. Top-quality posters can fetch between £5,000 and 20,000 or more. In contrast the market has become inundated with cartoon propaganda of little artistic merit and these images have little collectable value.

Condition of Russian posters is often very poor, because few have been looked after. Many have been mounted on wallpaper or rags and are in urgent need of restoration. Posters that have not been mounted should be put onto japan paper rather than linen.

Art Deco

The development of posters reflecting Europe's new streamlined style

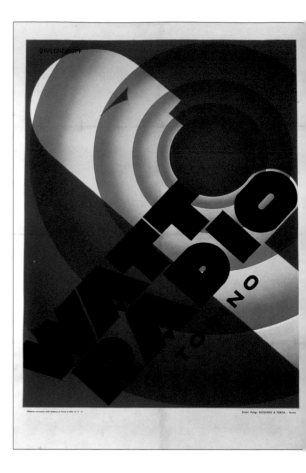

Art Deco is the generic term used to describe the decorative arts of the 1920s and 1930s. Inspired by the leading avant-garde artistic movements of the early 20th century such as Cubist painting and the architecture of the Bauhaus movement, Art Deco style dramatically affected the design of almost every aspect of the applied arts including furniture, ceramics, glass and metalwork.

In posters, as in other areas, the style is characterized by strong angular images and modern streamlined design. Posters of the time were varied, prolific and among the most visually striking ever made. Lettering became emphatically "modern" as new sans serif typesettings were used, and simplified typography played an increasingly important and integral role in the overall design, rather than being superimposed upon it. Colours were striking, chosen for maximum visual impact, and the influence of photography can be seen in the use of oblique viewpoints and dramatic perspective. Deco posters were also unprecedented for their simplicity; designers were not afraid to leave large areas of the poster blank to focus attention on the subject.

The subject matter of posters of this period reflects changes in modern society. Industrial development, new fashions and advances in transport were all frequently promoted by the poster designers of the day. Hence many posters of the period are for shipping, railways, motor cars and aviation. As methods of travel became easier and more widely available tourism became increasingly important and there are many posters advertising the delights of holiday resorts in England and on the Continent.

Sporting and leisure activities became increasingly important to the general public at this time, and poster designers were often commissioned to promote sporting events. The new clothes fashions of the "jazz age" were also illustrated in posters advertising stores and magazines. As with posters in the Art Nouveau style, the vast majority of Art Deco posters that survive were published in France, although many of the artists who flourished there were from other countries.

◀ **Nicolay Diulgheroff**
Poster advertising Watt Radio,
Torino, printed in 1933. The avant-
garde design reflects the influence
of abstract art. £500–800

▲ **Cassandre**
Etoile du Nord, printed in 1927. This
simple but striking design is one of
Cassandre's most famous creations.
£3,000–5,000

◀ **Roger Perot**
Poster advertising
Delahaye cars,
printed in 1932 by
Les Ateliers A.B.C.,
Paris. £3,000–4,000

One of the most highly influential and prolific poster designers was Adolphe Jean-Marie Mouron, better known as Cassandre. Cassandre was born in Russia and settled in Versailles, working extensively in Paris. His designs are distinctive for their absence of obvious decorative allure – unlike in Art Nouveau posters, there are virtually no languidly posed female figures. Instead Cassandre relied on abstract design and shape to create visual impact and his posters often reveal a highly innovative approach to advertising. A famous poster for Dubonnet designed by Cassandre in 1934 unusually illustrates the effect of the drink rather than the product itself, and shows the influence of Cubism on his original designs. A male figure clearly derived from Cubist art is repeated three times. The figure is shown drinking from a glass; as he drinks he is pervaded by colour as is the lettering – the progression reads *DUBO, DUBON, DUBONNET*.

Another famous design for the French railway, the *Etoile du Nord*, is perhaps his most dramatic. The train is not shown, and the poster is comprised of an abstract pattern of railway lines cutting through the landscape, with a star, representing the name of the railway, at the top. Cassandre made numerous posters for the railways, of which the rarest is his design for L.M.S., the British line London, Midland, Scotland, made in 1928; other classic designs were made for shipping such as the liner *SS Normandie* (see also p110–113).

Cassandre is probably the most popular and sought after of all Art Deco poster designers. Prices depend upon the appeal of the image and its rarity, as well as the usual criteria of condition and size. His later work was less distinctively "Art Deco" in style and is far less valuable. Cassandre's most famous images have been reprinted, although these will usually be identifiable by the fact that they are on the wrong paper. Fakes in his style and signed in the poster with his name have also been known. Cassandre's posters were printed by various firms including Alliance Graphique, Paris; Hachard & Cie, Paris; Draeger, Paris; L. Danel, Lille; Sauberlin & Pfeiffer S. A., Vevey; Coen & Cie, Milan.

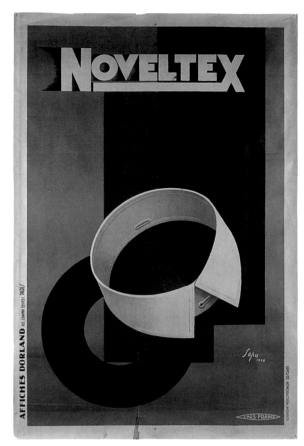

▶ **Paul Colin**
Poster advertising a performance by the celebrated dancer Serge Lifar.
£2,500–3,500

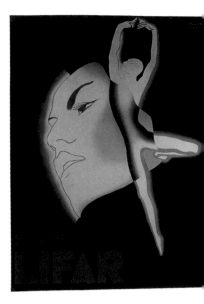

▼ **Leonetto Cappiello**
Poster advertising the newspaper *Le Petit Dauphinois*. The use of simple linear images and innovative design is a hallmark of Cappiello's best work. **£4,000–6,000**

▲ **Sepo (Severo Pozzati)**
Noveltex poster printed in Paris, 1928. The simple composition reflects the influence of Cubist collage. **£500–800**

A contemporary of Cassandre's, whose poster designs of the 1920s and 1930s reflect the influence of both Cubism and Surrealism, is Paul Colin. Colin's posters encompass a wide range of subjects, including festivals, shipping, theatrical productions and exhibitions. His work tends to be less angular and dramatic than Cassandre's and designs are often busier with more typography. His best work is none the less stylish and effective. His poster for *La Nuit de Paris* is inspired by collage in its stylized figures with Parisian monuments replacing features on the male spectator; another for the dancer Serge Lifar is a striking composition showing a dancing figure silhouetted against a linear, spotlit portrait with lettering in red. Colin's best work is highly sought after by collectors although it is less valuable than Cassandre's. Less appealing images are very modestly priced and later work which is less distinctively "deco" in effect is less desirable.

Another leading designer of Art Deco posters was Charles Gesmar who designed posters for several important Parisian music halls and theatres including the Folies Bergères and also turned his hand to costume design. Some of his most famous works were those produced in the 1920s for the renowned music hall singer Mistinguett. Numerous less well-known artists also worked in France producing highly decorative posters in the Art Deco style, and their work is generally available on the market today at modest prices. Among the less famous artists is Severo Pozzati, who signed his designs "Sepo" and produced posters for numerous brands of cigarette in the late 1920s and 1930s, many of them clearly inspired by Cubist collages.

Although the surviving Art Deco-style posters from other European countries are less widely available, the work of numerous accomplished artists and designers across the Continent reflected the new style. Some

◄ **Christopher Richard Wynne Nevinson**
English poster advertising the 1925 Wembley Exhibition.
The design is extremely colourful and the costumes of
the elegant female figures reflect the influence of
fashionable Japanese design. **£800–1200**

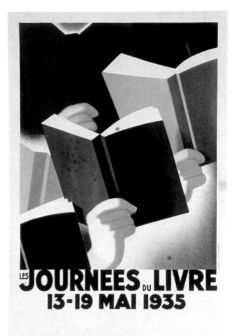

▲ **Paul Colin**
Les Journées du Livre, a striking Art Deco design
printed in 1935 by Serre & Cie. This example was
slightly damaged, hence the relatively low price. **£300–500**

dramatic posters were commissioned by
Dutch shipping lines. W. Ten Broek's poster
for the Holland-America Line in 1936 (see
p113) is clearly influenced by Cassandre – the
prow of the liner carves diagonally across the
design and the text is kept to a minimum.

In England many of the best posters of the
1920s and 1930s were commissioned by
London Underground, London Transport
and railway lines such as L.M.S. (see p107),
G.W.R. (Great Western Railway) and
L.N.E.R. (London North Eastern Railway).
Many designers were also commissioned by
Shell Oil to create posters, and the plethora of
good designs that survive compared with
other subjects is certainly a reflection of the
enlightened art directors who commissioned
the posters (see pp122). Among the work of
less well-known artists whose output is none
the less strikingly effective, is a dramatic
underground poster *No Wet No Cold* printed
in 1929 by Manner (see p115). This simply

comprised monochromatic umbrellas in the
rain. Other British designers who worked in
the modern style include Ashley Havinden,
Stanislaus Longley and Horace Taylor.

In Germany Art Deco was interpreted
in a more forceful nationalistic style in which
decorative qualities were less prominent.
Leading artists include Ludwig Hohlwein,
whose numerous designs produced between
1910 and the mid-1930s reflect the developing
German style. In Switzerland a distinctive
version of the Art Deco style emerged in the
work of artists such as Augusto Giacometti,
Niklaus Stoecklin and Otto Baumberger.
Subjects covered include travel and the
clothes store PK2. For collectors of Swiss
posters, condition is crucial; unlike other
posters Swiss examples should not be linen-
backed, although japan paper backing is
acceptable. While good Swiss posters in
good condition can fetch very high prices
at auction, most are in the mid-price range.

Transport

Posters advertising trains, shipping, aeroplanes, London Underground, cars and bicycles

▲ Cassandre
Chemin de Fer du Nord was printed in 1929
to advertise the French railway company.
£2,000–3,000

► Terence Cune
*Scotland for yo
Holidays*, a post
advertising Briti
Rail showing
train crossing t
Forth Bridg
printed c.195
Cuneo is kno
for the accura
and detail of h
train posters a
is keenly collecte
£300–5

The meteoric technological advancements in all methods of transportation in the 20th century have given rise to a wealth of fascinating posters. As new methods of transport evolved and others improved, posters played a key role in increasing public awareness of these newly available and often luxurious modes of transport. Railway companies, shipping lines, and manufacturers of motor cars, bicycles and aeroplanes all quickly realized the potential of advertising and turned to posters to publicize their services. For the most part these images were produced in relatively limited quantities and as they quickly became outdated were replaced by others. Today their appeal lies in the fascinating detail of travel from a bygone age, and they remain keenly sought after by transport enthusiasts as well as general poster collectors.

In style, transport posters reflect the age in which they were made, and some of the most valuable and charming images are those reflecting the prevailing trends of Art Nouveau and Art Deco design. A wide range of artists both well known and obscure turned their hand to designing transport posters and, with a few notable exceptions, the design of the poster is usually more important than the name of the artist. Posters featuring figures clad in period costume together with the machines they are advertising are usually more interesting and therefore more valuable than those in which there is just an empty landscape.

Among the earliest transport posters are those commissioned by the various regional railways that made travelling increasingly accessible to the masses in the early decades of the 20th century. In Britain the four leading railway companies who commissioned posters were G.W.R. (Great Western Railway), L.N.E.R. (London & North Eastern Railway), L.M.S. (London, Midland, Scotland) and Southern Railway. Posters also proliferated in France where among the leading companies were L'Oiseau Bleu, P.L.M. (Paris, Lyon, Mediterrannée) and Chemin de Fer du Nord.

THE WORLD FAMOUS FORTH BRIDGE

SCOTLAND FOR YOUR HOLIDAYS

Services and fares from **BRITISH RAILWAYS** stations, offices and agencies

Railway posters made their first appearance around 1900 in Europe, where they flourished for the next three decades. Their heyday in Britain was from 1923 until 1947, when the nationalization of the railways brought about their gradual demise.

Railway posters fall into two main groups: those sponsored by the railway companies showing the various regions, towns and cities which the traveller could reach by taking the train (discussed in the section on tourism), and those in which the railway or a train forms the subject of the image. The most valuable are by the leading Art Deco poster designer Cassandre (see pp106–9), who designed numerous railway posters in the 1920s and 1930s for French and British companies. His rarest and most valuable train poster was made for a British company and was entitled *LMS Bestway*. Other less rare but still highly desirable railway subjects by Cassandre include designs for the Nord Express, Chemin de Fer du Nord and L'Oiseau Bleu. The posters are characterized by the angularity of

the designs, unusual viewpoints and dramatic use of typography and line to create visual impact. Others who designed for the French railways include Julien Lacaze, Roger Broders who only designed for P.L.M., Hugo d'Alesi, Albert Brenet and Louis Tauzin.

Frank Pick, general manager of London Underground, helped many young artists in Britain to establish their reputations by commissioning designs from them, an example followed by many of the railway companies. Among the artists associated with work in this area are Tom Purvis, Frank Newbold and Terence Cuneo, but other well-known artists also designed railway posters, including Laura Knight and Frank Brangwyn. Cuneo's posters are admired by railway enthusiasts for their accuracy, and his best date from 1949 to the early 1960s. Later designs are usually signed both with his name and with his "signature" mouse, although this does not appear on early images. Prices for much of his work still seem relatively low given the quality.

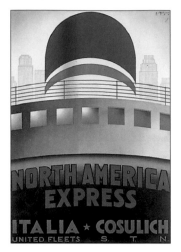

◀ S. Patrone
Italian shipping poster reflecting the influence of Art Deco modernity. This example was printed in Genoa in 1934. £500–800

▶ Montague Black
Posters advertising well known ships command a premium. This example for White Star Line, c.1912, mentions the ill-fated *Titanic* and is therefore especially valuable. £2000–3000

◀ Albert Sebille
An early example of a French shipping poster printed in 1912. The excellent quality boosts the value. £1,000–2,000

Shipping

Shipping posters, redolent of a means of travel that has now largely disappeared, have long been highly sought after for their nostalgic appeal. From the closing decades of the 19th century onwards these stylish and evocative posters were commissioned by all the major international shipping lines for display in travel agencies and booking offices. The designs typically emphasized the luxury of the liner, the power and speed of which it was capable, the fashionable world in which you would mingle as you travelled, and the far-flung destinations to which you would be transported.

In Britain the leading shipping companies included: P&O, Cunard, Red Star, White Star, Canadian Pacific and Union Castle; while in Europe, North America and Canada posters were made for companies such as Holland-America Line, Italia, Fabre Lines, Messageries Maritimes, Compagnie Générale Transatlantique, United States Lines and Canadian Pacific. The majority of posters date from 1900 to the 1950s although earlier and later examples are sometimes seen.

Stylistically, shipping posters reflect the period in which they were made. Earlier examples tended to incorporate far more lettering and far more detailed illustrative techniques. Some posters were almost covered with writing and illustrated only by a small vignette of the ship and perhaps the destinations it visited; others showed the liner at full steam ahead, sometimes framed with fluttering flags or towering above a smaller vessel, and often with admiring spectators looking on. Many were unsigned, but among the better-known designers of shipping posters from around the turn of the century are Hugo d'Alesi who designed a poster for Compagnie Générale Transatlantique for their New York-Lehavre route; Henri Cassiers, a Belgian artist, who designed posters for Red Star Line in the late 19th and early 20th centuries, and Odin Rosenvinge, whose posters for the Cunard Line ships including the *Lusitania* and *Mauritania* date from c.1905 to the 1930s.

Among the most striking and valuable shipping posters are those in the Art Deco style. The famous

French poster designer Cassandre is best-known for his posters for the palatial Art Deco liner *Normandie*, which can fetch high prices. Similarly dramatic designs, probably influenced by Cassandre, were made by the Dutch poster designer Willem Ten Broek. His poster for the Holland-America Line (1936) shows the imposing prow of the liner looming dominantly over the entire surface of the composition (see above).

Among the most prolific designers of shipping posters in the 1930s and 1940s was Albert Sebille who made many posters for Compagnie Générale Transatlantique (see facing page). Another equally accomplished artist was Georges Taboreau, who under the pseudonym Sandy Hook designed posters for Messageries Maritimes and Compagnie Générale Transatlantique between c.1910 and 1950. In England, although most shipping posters were unsigned, some well-known artists produced them on occasions. These include Terence Cuneo, best known for his train posters (see p111), and the maritime artists Norman Wilkinson, who made posters for Canadian Pacific's liner *Montcalm*, and C. E. Turner, who designed posters for Cunard.

Kenneth Shoesmith also made posters in London in the 1930s for Canadian Pacific liners to Canada and the USA. In the 1950s, as travel by sea maintained its popularity, posters for liners continued to abound. One artist who stands out in this period is Albert Brenet who designed posters for Messageries Maritimes and Compagnie Générale Transatlantique, some featuring a female figure in national costume with the liner in the background.

As with other forms of poster, the impact of the image is fundamental in establishing value. Collectors prefer designs in which the ship plays an important part the overall design and looks as imposing as possible. The most highly prized examples are those for the luxurious transatlantic liners of the day. Those featuring famous liners such as the French ships *Normandie* and *France* or the *Lusitania* and *Mauritania* are particularly valuable. Posters for the ill-fated *Titanic* are also keenly collected and always command a premium.

-KEEPS LONDON GOING

▲ Man Ray
The most valuable of all London Underground posters to date is this rare example designed in 1939 by the famous Surrealist artist. **£15,000–20,000**

► Dora Batty
Poster for London Underground, printed in 1925. The drab colouring reduces value but the attractively dressed figure adds to the poster's appeal.
£400–600

◄ Tony Sarg
'Appy 'Ampstead by the Underground, an amusing design printed in 1913 and packed with anecdotal detail.
£300–500

London Transport Posters

Produced in huge variety by many of the leading British and international artists of the day, posters made for London's Underground and buses date from the early years of the 20th century and rank among the most innovative and interesting transport posters ever made. Although no longer commissioned by London Transport in such quantity, the tradition is still continued to some extent today and contemporary posters are also increasingly collectable.

The birth of London Transport posters was due largely to the artistic insight of the general manager of the London Underground, Frank Pick. Pick was made responsible for improving the poor image of London Underground. A keen patron of the industrial arts, with an innovative approach to design, he realized the wall space in Underground tunnels not rented to other advertisers could be used

to provide a means of illustrating the multitude of destinations that London's Underground and buses made available. In doing so he encouraged numerous artists to design for him. In 1916 he also commissioned Edward Johnston to create a new typeface for his posters: the first sanserif type of the 20th century.

London Underground and bus posters were used to illustrate a huge range of destinations in a similarly varied range of artistic styles. Attractions such as Kew Gardens and Regent's Park Zoo became the subject of numerous posters. Tony Sarg made a series of posters for Richmond Park, Hampstead and Southend (c.1913) featuring bird's-eye views populated with animated cartoon vignettes. Posters were also commissioned to advertise the way to get to important sporting venues, such as Wimbledon and Wembley, and to land-

▲ *No Wet No Cold*
Poster by Manner printed in
1929. The high value reflects
the accomplished design,
despite the designer being
little known. £1,000–1,500

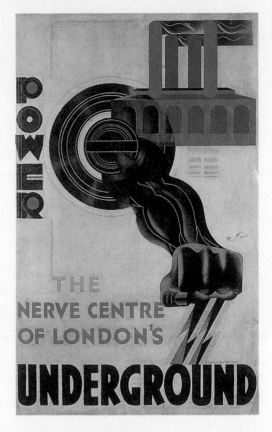

▲ **Edward McKnight Kauffer**
One of the artist's most striking designs for London
Underground, this poster was printed in 1931 by Vincent
Brooks Day & Sons. £6,000–8,000

marks such as the museums and art galleries. Designers included Edward McKnight Kauffer, Eric Ravilious, Betty Swanwick, Spencer Pryse, Frank Brangwyn, Rex Whistler, Sybil Andrews and Cyril Power and Christopher Richard Wynne Nevinson. A fascinating archive of Underground and transport posters is contained at the London Transport Museum, Covent Garden.

Prices for Underground posters depend on rarity and the artist concerned as well as the design, but collectors should be aware that reproductions of some early examples have also been published. The Surrealist artist Man Ray made one design featuring planets in space, reminiscent of the Underground logo. This rare example is among the most valuable of all Underground posters. Zoo subjects are also often highly appealing as are the most stylish and pictorial designs by less well-known artists.

Among the artists whom Pick encouraged to design for him, one of the most prolific and highly regarded was the American Edward McKnight Kauffer. Kauffer came to Europe in 1913 and began producing extremely stylish designs that represent a synthesis between elements of Cubism and Surrealism with the decorative qualities of Art Deco style. Prices for Kauffer's work vary according to the impact of the visual image. His less expensive transport posters include those for museums such as the Wallace Collection and the Indian Museum and pictorial designs such as *Spring* and *Autumn*. One of his most valuable posters is *Power, The Nerve Centre of London's Underground*, which shows a clenched fist emitting lightning and emerging from the Underground logo (see above). Kauffer also designed posters for Shell, Pan American, the C.A.A. and Great Western Railways.

▶ **Charles Rambert**
Grande Semaine d'Aviation, published in 1910 in Rouen. This is a typical example of a poster advertising an early air show. £1,200–1,500

▲ **Georges Hamel**
Poster advertising the 7th Monaco Grand Prix, printed in 1935 by Monégasque, Monte Carlo. £3,000–3,500

Cycling, Motoring & Aviation

For collectors on a limited budget the wealth of cycling posters made in the late 19th and early 20th centuries offers an opportunity to build a fascinating collection for relatively modest sums. Cycling was popular as a pastime as well as a means of transport, and posters for brands of bicycle were produced in vast numbers, particularly in France.

Among the manufacturers who feature in posters are Wolff bicycles, an American company (although the posters were printed in Paris), Wonder, Griffon, Rochet, Hurtu, Alcyon, Excelsior, Consul and Liberator. Notable artists who designed cycling posters include Misti (Ferdinand Mifliez) and Pal (Jean de Paléologue; even Toulouse-Lautrec (see p97) designed a poster advertising bicycles.

With the exception of Lautrec's poster, cycling subjects are for the most part more modestly priced than motoring posters, even though the most attractive, featuring fashionably clad figures cycling sedately in a landscape, have great nostalgic charm. Posters for motorcycles were also made from the 1920s. Monet Goyon, Ultima and Dresch are among those who commissioned posters in which speed or the mechanical intricacies of the machine are emphasized in the futuristic designs.

Posters advertising cars were produced from the early 1900s by numerous small manufacturers mostly of French cars. Early posters usually featured cars that were variants of the de Dion-Bouton and emphasized the glamour and exclusivity of motoring, showing the cars being sedately driven by fashionably clad figures. The names of many of these early manufacturers are nowadays obscure and include Suere, Martini, Brasier, Delahaye and Barry. As motoring became increasingly popular in the 1920s and 1930s speed became an increasingly important aspect of the design. As well as being produced fo car manufacturers, posters were also commissioned by motoring clubs, driving schools

◀ **Francisco Tamango**
A poster designed for Terrot & Cie advertising bicycles, published c.1910.
£300–500

▼ **Misti (Ferdinand Mifliez)**
Populaires de Dion-Bouton, a poster designed in 1903 advertising one of the earliest commercially manufactured motor cars. The elegant figures add to its appeal.
£1,800–2,000

▲ **Jersey Airways**
Anonymous poster advertising the airlink between Jersey and London and Southampton showing the planes landing on the beach. **£600–800**

and by manufacturers of accessories such as tyres by Pirelli, Michelin or Goodyear, or fuel by Le Sourd. Posters featuring the famous Michelin man have a particularly keen following.

The sense of speed and excitement of the race make motor racing posters among the most popular and valuable of all motoring posters. Grand Prix races featured in posters from the 1920s onwards and the most popular are those in which a sense of speed predominates in the design. Key artists of early racing posters are Geo Ham (Georges Hamel, who also sometimes signed as Geo Matt) and Robert Falcucci, both of whom designed posters for the Monaco Grand Prix and Rallies in the 1930s and 1940s. Their colourful and imposing designs are keenly collected although the market has vacillated in recent years in tandem with the fluctuations in prices in the vintage car market. Motoring posters of the 1940s, 1950s and 1960s tend to reflect the increasing accessibility of the car. Many posters advertise

cars by manufacturers such as Ford, Humber, Peugeot, Renault and Audi. These tend to be less popular than posters for more exclusive names unless the image has particular period appeal.

The earliest aeronautical posters tend to advertise air shows and exhibitions, and airships and aeroplanes also often appear in the backgrounds of posters for other products. The emerging commercial airlines begin to feature in posters from the 1930s, and as air travel became more readily available in the 1950s and 1960s, posters were made in increasing numbers to advertise airlines such as B.E.A., B.O.A.C. and Pan-Am. Posters for defunct airlines are especially popular; the most desirable tend to be those showing the aircraft in some detail, perhaps with a cutout view of the interior. Posters advertising unusual air routes and smaller airlines are also much coveted; for example there is a keen following for early Jersey Airways posters which show the planes landing on the beach (see above).

Travel & Tourism

Collecting posters advertising domestic and exotic holiday destinations and how to get there

▲ **Hugo d'Alesi**
Turn-of-the-century poster advertising the spa town of Vittel, which could be reached from Paris in 5½ hours by train. **£200–400**

Apart from advertisements for consumer commodities and theatrical productions, travel and tourism accounts for the bulk of posters made in the late 19th and early 20th centuries. Developments in transport went hand in hand with expanding public transport systems and as travel improved, holidays in resorts at home or abroad became increasingly accessible. Throughout mainland Europe and Great Britain large numbers of tourist posters were produced to advertise the delights of towns, cities, mountains and coastal attractions. Many tourism posters were commissioned by the railways as a way of showing people how rail services were now bringing previously inaccessible destinations within their reach, and offering special prices on tickets. Others were commissioned by the municipal authorities or by hoteliers to inform the public of the wealth of leisure pursuits available in any particular area.

As with transport posters, travel posters are often unsigned or by little-known commercial artists, and with such an abundance of tourist and travel material available, subject matter and decorative appeal are all-important in establishing value. The most desirable subjects are those showing well-dressed figures in fashionable locations. Rustic figures or deserted landscapes with no figures at all are usually far less interesting and consequently do not command such high prices. Other factors that can affect the price include the location itself. Places which are still popular tourist destinations today, such as the southern French resorts or Alpine ski resorts are in higher demand by collectors than those for more obscure places. The incidental detail contained in a poster, such as local scenery or period costume, can also contribute greatly to a its appeal. The value of a poster can double if the figures it contains are shown playing a popular sport such as golf

▼ **Belgian seaside posters**
An anonymous poster for the northern Belgian coast, c.1920. This example is more valuable than most because of its period detail. **£800–1,200**

▲ **Anton Reckziegel**
Vierwaldstätter-See, an early 20th-century Swiss poster, typically includes a panoramic view and a train timetable. **£400–600**

or beach tennis. Tourism posters started to appear from the 1880s when they were often used to advertise fashionable spa and coastal towns. Early examples in the flowery Art Nouveau style often feature detailed landscapes and elaborately dressed and coiffed figures, sometimes partially framed with elaborate cartouches. Lettering is also often highly stylized and it is not uncommon to see several different typefaces used in the same design, all of which adds to the overall effect of rich if fussy design.

Early travel posters were produced in considerable quantity particularly in Belgium, where they were used to promote the fashionable, if dubious, delights of northern coastal resorts such as Ostend, Heyst, Nieuport, St Idesbald Plage and Wenduyne, as well as spas such as Liège and Val d'Amblève and the cultural attractions of Brussels. Most of the artists of Belgian posters are not well known but among the more

prolific artists are Roland Florizoone, Armand Rassenfosse, Leo Marfut and Eduard Duych. Prices for Belgian posters are generally low unless the subject matter is particularly appealing.

In Switzerland tourist posters were made for towns, mountain regions and skiing resorts. Switzerland operated a huge railway system and many posters were sponsored by the rail networks. Early Swiss posters were mainly timetables for trains, and these are usually less decorative and therefore less valuable than those from the 1920s onwards in more distinctive styles. Demand is particularly high for posters for desirable mountain resorts such as Davos, Gstaad, St Moritz and Zermatt (see p129); posters were also made for cities and lakeside resorts such as Geneva and Lugano and these are often more modestly priced. Many Swiss posters were also commissioned by grand hotels; those showing figures playing golf are particularly sought after.

◀ **Costantini**
Italian poster, c.1900,
advertising the Grand
Hotel des Thermes,
Salsomaggiore. £600–800

▲ **Frank Mason**
Travel poster printed in 1948,
commissioned by British Rail
to advertise Southend-on-Sea,
Essex. The picture postcard
style is a feature of many
British tourist posters.
£200–400

▶ **Georges Doriva**
Tourist posters that includ
sporting scenes alway
command a premium. Th
golfing scene makes thi
poster of c.1910 advertisin
the French resort of Etreta
extremely sought afte
£1,000–1,50

Because most commissions for later Swiss posters were awarded by competition, designs were often extremely innovative and of exceptionally high standard. Among the most keenly collected Swiss poster artists are Otto Marach, who designed very striking futuristic posters for the Bremgarten railway; Herbert Matter, who made use of photomontage and lithography in his avant-garde designs; and Niklaus Stoecklin who also did futuristic designs from the 1940s onwards. Other artists who made posters for Swiss resorts include Herbert Leupin, Augusto Giacometti, Otto Bauberger and Emil Cardinaux. Swiss posters are always on top-quality paper and although they are less abundant than French posters the artists are usually well documented.

As with Swiss posters those made for Italian resorts were mostly commissioned by railway networks. Italian travel posters tend to be less avidly collected than Italian posters for fashion – once again value relies heavily on the town or region concerned. Posters advertising northern towns such as Turin,

attractions such as the lakes, or resorts such as Capri are popular, but posters for southern towns are usually far less valuable.

In Britain, as elsewhere, travel posters showed the huge range of places that could be reached by taking advantage of the improving transport systems. Early English tourist posters often incorporate an element of humour that was rarely seen in mainland Europe, but the vast majority of English tourism posters date from the 1920s onwards. Compared with their continental counterparts English tourist posters of the 1930s are less stylized and often highly pictorial in style, rather like painted postcards. Posters of this time typically showed a panoramic view of the landscape or resort with its title emblazoned in a separate band underneath alongside the name or logo of the sponsoring transport company. There is often no attempt at all to link the lettering with the image.

In contrast to the rather straightforward approach of British travel posters were the extraordinarily stylish creations of French

Collecting
Roger Broders

artists. Monte Carlo, Corsica, Antibes, Nice and St Malo were among the French tourist attractions promoted in poster designs. Posters were also made to promote events such as the famous flower festivals, as well as fashionable casinos and grand hotels such as the Cashat Majestic, Chamonix or the Negresco, Nice. Among the host of artists who produced posters from the turn of the century are Hugo d'Alesi who made posters for Cannes and elsewhere (including Switzerland); René Péan, whose turn-of-the-century-style posters feature elegantly clad women on the beaches of St Malo or on the boat train to England; and Raymond Tournon who designed posters for Dieppe and Enghien around the same time and in similar style. French posters from the 1920s and 1930s reflect the new approach to decorative graphics, with strong, linear designs, and flat areas of colour. The leading travel poster designer of this time was Roger Broders but Georges Dorival and Julien Lacaze also produced some dashing examples epitomizing the elegance of Art Deco style.

Roger Broders designed stylish images of the fashionable resorts of the 1920s and 1930s, and these are among the most avidly collected of all travel posters. His designs are typically highly simplified, relying on the use of line, bright colours and a minimal use of modern lettering to create strong visual impact. Compositions often feature fashionably clad, elongated figures. Sought-after designs include those for Riviera resorts such as Juan-les-Pins, Ste Maxime and Villefranche. Less colourful subjects and designs with no figures are much less desirable and are modestly priced. Value is also affected by the rarity of the particular poster. Posters for Dunkerque, Calvi and Golden Mountain Express are rarely seen and therefore attract higher prices. Most of Broders' posters were published by Lucien Serre, who specialized in tourist posters, although Broders also used other Parisian printers including J. Langlois, Pierre Lafitte, Imprimerie Vaugirard and Imprimerie Monégasque. Dimensions reflect the sizes required for billboards. (Most pre-1928 examples measure 31 x 42in/75 x 108cm, later ones 25 x 39in/ 64 x 100cm.)

Shell Posters

Among the most interesting and diverse British posters produced from the 1920s onwards are those made to promote the Shell Oil company. Shell's early posters of the 1920s were rather predictable in style and content, typically showing cans of fuel, perhaps accompanied by biplanes or racing cars. Early designers of Shell posters include Tom Purvis, who continued to contribute designs throughout the 1930s, and the cartoonist illustrator H. M. Bateman. Bateman's poster for Shell incorporated a characteristic element of humour. Entitled *Concentration* it showed a well-dressed gentleman filling his smart car with Shell oil from a canister, oblivious to the fact that behind him an unscrupulous crook was ˙sneaking up to snatch a second unguarded can of oil.

The most innovative Shell posters date from the 1930s when the responsibility for Shell's advertising was assumed by Jack Beddington. Under his direction an increasingly illustrious list of artists was commissioned to design posters for Shell. Beddington's idea was to promote the company's image in a rather more subtle way than had hitherto been the norm. Instead of simply illustrating the product or the machines that used it, Beddington looked at other alternative ways to advertise his product. One long-lasting campaign focused on the British landmarks you could reach using Shell petrol and became one of Shell's most effective methods of advertising, continuing until the 1950s. The posters were appropriately displayed on the sides of delivery lorries which carried fuel to petrol stations throughout the country.

Beddington was not afraid to draw on the most famous avant-garde artists of the 1930s to help in these campaigns: Vanessa Bell designed a poster showing a pointillistic view of Alfriston with the caption *See Britain First on Shell* in 1931, while the same year, McKnight Kauffer designed striking posters showing the New Forest, Stonehenge and

You can be sure of Shell, Brimham Rock, Yorkshire shows how effective Sutherland's distinctively bold but romantic approach to landscape could be adapted to poster design. **£400–600**

▼ **Mary Kessell**
The value of posters by less well-known artists relies on the desirability of the location. The Cotswold scene featured in *You can be sure of Shell: Arlington Row, Bibury* would be a fairly popular subject. **£200–400**

▲ **John Armstrong**
A striking design from the "These Men Use Shell" campaign. This poster is subtitled *Farmers*.
£300–500

Bodiam Castle with the same caption. Graham Sutherland depicted the oast houses of Kent, and the Great Globe, Swanage framed with the words *Everywhere you go you can be sure of Shell*, in 1932, and this slogan, along with *To visit Britain's landmarks you can be sure of Shell*, continued to be used until the 1950s. Paul Nash interpreted the Rye Marshes in a geometric style in 1932 and Kimmeridge Folly, Dorset in 1937.

Beddington's other important theme concentrated on people of various professions who relied upon Shell products. As with the British landmarks theme, people "who prefer Shell" included a similarly extraordinary range of subjects and styles. Antiquaries and anglers were depicted by C. & R. Ellis in 1934; artists were illustrated by John Armstrong in 1933; gardeners were shown by Cedric Morris in 1934; seamen and tourists by Tristram Hillier in 1934 and 1936; film stars by Cathleen Mann in 1938; and motorists by J. S.

Anderson in 1935. There were also posters of mobile police, sightseers, farmers, racing motorists, journalists and many more.

Most of the Shell posters that formed part of the Beddington advertising campaigns in the 1930s were highly pictorial, with the lettering used merely to frame the image rather than playing any part in the design itself. Apart from this format there are few similarities of artistic style and with such an eclectic mix of artists, artistic styles vary widely, ranging from straightforward pictorial images to Cubist designs and Surrealistic compositions.

Value for Shell posters depends on the reputation of the artist, the graphics and the date. Early examples by leading artists are keenly collected although, compared with prices for works by the leading French designers, Shell posters still seem relatively undervalued, and offer collectors the rare chance to buy images designed by leading avant-garde artists relatively inexpensively.

Sport

Posters promoting popular sporting events, resorts and venues

Perennially popular with collectors, sports posters were made to promote important competitions, to advertise sporting equipment, or to show the public how to get to important sporting events using public transport. Amateur sports also often feature as background detail in travel and tourism posters and, because of the limited availability of sporting subject matter, these are also much sought after. Apart from posters for winter sports and some Olympic posters, which were occasionally designed by well-known artists, most sporting subjects are by relatively unknown designers, and in general it is the subject rather than the artist which is of major concern to collectors. Many collectors of sporting posters are themselves enthusiasts of the sport; thus posters featuring sports which are popular today, such as golf and tennis, are especially avidly sought after and can fetch surprisingly high sums for even run-of-the-mill examples. The most prized sporting posters are examples from the late

19th and early decades of the 20th centuries, but compared with other collecting areas such as shipping, motoring and travel virtually all types of pre-1960 sporting posters are relatively rare and therefore of some value.

Tennis posters are extremely popular with collectors in the UK and posters have been made for Wimbledon championships and Davis Cup tournaments as well as manufacturers of tennis rackets and balls such as Dunlop. Many of the posters for Wimbledon were sponsored by London Underground. Tennis as played by amateur enthusiasts is also sometimes featured in the background of French and Belgian tourist posters.

Golf as a fashionable pastime became especially popular from the turn of the century and posters for a wide variety of products often incorporate golf in their advertising posters to add to the image of exclusivity of the product. Golf often features in the background of British and some French railway posters and frequently appears in the

◀ **Paul Nash**
Footballers prefer Shell, c.1937, a rare football poster that formed part of Shell Oil's long-standing campaign showing the various occupations "who prefer Shell" (see also p122).
£1,000–1,500

◀ **Tom Eckersley and Eric Lombers**
This poster advertising the 1935 Wimbledon championships was commissioned by London Transport.
£300–500

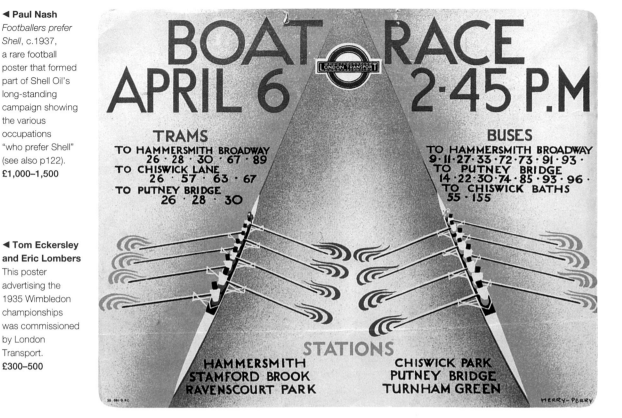

▲ **Heather Perry**
Poster advertising the 1935 Oxford/Cambridge University Boat Race, commissioned by London Underground. £150–250

background of Swiss tourist posters. Roger Broders' poster for Vichy commissioned by P.L.M. included both a figure playing golf and a tennis net and ball to indicate the fashionable sports one could enjoy in the region. Such is the demand for golfing posters that even modern posters are collected. Those for St Andrews Golf Club in Scotland are much sought after but extremely rare, as are posters for important American competitions such as the US Open.

Even rarer than golfing and tennis posters are those for early football and rugby events. As a general rule football posters are less keenly collected than those for rugby, golf or tennis and prices tend to be lower. The most valuable football posters date from before the 1940s. Recent posters for the World Cup are generally widely available and not very valuable. One of the most innovatively designed British footballing posters is by Paul Nash, commissioned by Shell Oil; part of a campaign, the caption reads *Footballers prefer*

Shell. Rugby posters are a newer collecting area and even posters for recent events are rising in value. There is a newly established museum at Twickenham where an archive of rugby posters can be seen.

Rowing posters are also much collected and rare. Most were produced in England where the sport was particularly popular, and posters for the famous boat race were commissioned by London Transport. In Germany posters for rowing competitions were also produced in the 1930s and these are also worth looking out for.

Among the host of other sporting pursuits that are featured in posters, boxing has a keen following with collectors. Price for boxing posters depends not only on the usual criteria of date and rarity but also on the reputation of the boxer and on the importance of the sporting event they promote. Early examples are much collected but even posters from the 1950s and 1960s can fetch surprisingly high sums if the fight is a notable one.

▶ **Yusaku Kamekura**
A simple but striking poster designed for the Tokyo Olympics in 1964. **£800–1,200**

▲ **Olle Hjortzberg**
Designed for the Stockholm Olympics of 1912, this is the earliest recorded poster for the games, and one of the most valuable. **£1,600–1,900**

▼ **John Sjosvard**
Poster for the 1956 Stockholm Olympics, featuring a monumental equestrian figure. **£400–600**

The Olympics

Early posters for the Olympic games are extremely popular with collectors and can fetch thousands of pounds, but with few exceptions those for recent games tend as yet to be too widely available to be very valuable. In general it is the rarity of the particular poster rather than the artist or the design which has the greatest bearing on value.

The first modern Olympic games were held in Athens in 1896, following the establishment of the Olympic committee by Baron Pierre de Coubertin in 1894. But although covers from early programmes of events survive (and are included in sales of posters), the earliest true advertising poster for the games to survive is that designed by Olle Hjortzberg for the 1912 Olympics held in Stockholm. As with many Olympic posters, the

artist was relatively unknown but a native of the country in which the games were taking place. Another early and valuable poster dates from 1914; designed by Edouard Elzingre, it was published in Geneva to mark the 20th anniversary of the reestablishment of the games.

Posters from the Olympics of the 1920s and 1930s are all relatively rare and much coveted, mostly falling in the mid-hundreds of pounds price range. Particularly popular are posters for the 10th Olympic games held in 1932 in Los Angeles, such as the example by Julio Kilenyi. This is interesting from the design point of view since it incorporates the avant-garde photomontage technique, and this factor coupled with the rarity of the poster and the American location all combine to boost the price

▼ **Jean Droit**
A rare poster designed
for the 8th Olympic
games held in 1924 in
Paris. **£3,000–4,000**

▲ **Edouard Elzingre**
Marking the 20th
anniversary of the
reestablishment of
the modern Olympic
games, this poster
was published in
Switzerland in 1914.
£800–1,200

considerably. Posters for the winter Olympics are also keenly collected, having first appeared in 1924. Among the more commonly seen winter games posters are those for Grenoble 1968, and Lake Placid 1980 (for which Robert Whitney and Howard E. Jennings produced designs).

Olympic posters reflect a huge choice of artistic styles ranging from highly abstract designs to pictorial or photographic images featuring the various sports, such as football, gymnastics and swimming. All styles of poster have their followers. The abstract poster designed by Yusaku Kamekura for the Tokyo Olympics of 1964 is extremely popular; depicting only the red sun of Japan, the Olympic symbol of interlinked circles and the words "Tokyo 1964", it can still fetch sums of well over £1,000.

Posters for more recent Olympics have survived in substantial quantities, and usually fetch modest sums, even though some designs were by extremely famous artists. For the 1972 Munich Olympics, Oscar Kokoschka, Marino Marini, David Hockney, Victor Vasarely and R. B. Kitaj were among the leading names to produce designs for posters. There are so many examples of these posters surviving that at auction they are often sold in multiple lots. For the 1984 Los Angeles Olympics artists such as Robert Rauschenberg, Martin Puryear, Jonathan Borofsky, Billy Al Bengston, R. Saunders, John Baldessari and Garry Winogrand were commissioned to make designs. These too are very modestly priced, as are posters designed for the 1994 Olympics in Barcelona.

▼ Anton Reckziegel
Typical of the earlier posters promoting skiing areas, this highly detailed design, published in 1899, includes a train timetable. **£200–400**

◄ Roger Broders
Like many of Broders' travel posters, this example for St Gervais-les-Bains was commissioned by P.L.M., the French railway company. All Broders' designs are keenly sought after, and in this case the skiing subject matter adds a premium. **£500–800**

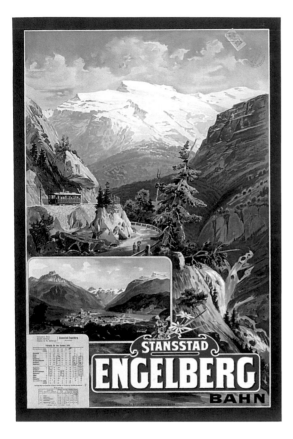

► Walter Koch
A poster promoting ice skating at Davos, Switzerland, published in 1922. The striking design is typical of the best posters of this decade. **£1,000–1,200**

Winter Sports

Winter sports posters are highly popular with today's ski enthusiasts and appeal both for their decorative qualities and as a fascinating record of the evolution of winter sports. A collection of skiing posters spanning the 20th century will provide an interesting insight into how early equipment made from materials such as wood and seal skins was gradually refined, and early images have great nostalgic appeal.

Winter sports posters first appeared at the turn of the century and have been produced in increasing numbers as the popularity of winter sports has grown. The vast majority were produced for the Swiss and French Alpine resorts, and provided advertising not only for towns but also equipment, clothing and events. Posters featuring winter sports in countries such as Spain, Germany, Finland and Sweden are generally far scarcer although no more

valuable. Winter sports are also sometimes featured in posters advertising other commodities, a factor which as with other sports can dramatically boost their value. Many winter sports posters were commissioned by the railway systems and were designed to show you how you could get to these newly fashionable locations.

Posters from the turn of the century are usually highly detailed in design, often featuring several vignette landscapes, lots of lettering and sometimes incorporating a train timetable – all of which tends to reduce their visual impact. As a result, despite their relative rarity, these very early examples tend to be less valuable than the most striking designs of the 1920s and 1930s, which encapsulate the elegance, exclusivity and sophistication of skiing.

The value of winter sporting posters is also dramatically affected by the location they show. Resorts

SPORTS D'HIVER à CHAMONIX

CACHAT'S-MAJESTIC

Atelier FARIA 16, Rue Clignancourt - TCL ☒ PARIS

▲ **Candido Aragonese de Faria**
Poster for a leading Alpine hotel; the elegant figures add visual appeal. £1000–1500

which are still fashionable and where wealthy collectors have homes today tend to attract the highest sums, as many collectors like to buy posters of the regions in which they live. For this reason posters showing resorts such as Zermatt, Davos, Chamonix, St Moritz and Gstaad command a premium, while there is far less demand for those depicting the Pyrenees and Jura regions. Demand is also strong for posters showing hotels such as the Palace Hotel, St Moritz or Cashat's Majestic, Chamonix.

Although skiing is the activity most commonly featured in winter sports posters, they also represent a surprising range of other sporting pastimes including ice skating, mountaineering, bob sleighing, sledging, tobogganing, ice hockey, snow boarding – a sport which featured in posters of the 1930s – and even horse racing on the snow – a special event held at St Moritz.

One of the artists most associated with posters for winter sports is Anton Reckziegel who in the first decade of the 20th century designed posters for the Swiss railways featuring the mountainous landscape through which the trains passed. In the 1920s and 1930s Roger Broders' prolific output of travel posters included designs for Saint Gervais les Bains and St Pierre de Chartreuse. Also highly sought after is a poster designed by Otto Morach for Davos. Other artists who can attract considerable sums include Emil Cardinaux, who designed posters for the Jungfrau railway; Burkhard Mangold, who made an extremely valuable design for PKZ confectionery showing men tobogganing; and Walter Koch whose design for an ice skating race in Davos also attracts high prices. René Péan, Henri Tanconville, Roger Soubie and Louis Tauzin are also worth looking out for.

Theatre
& the
performing
arts

Collecting posters for theatrical and operatic productions, actors, singers, dancers and the circus

◄ **Tito Corbella**
A poster for *Tosca* printed c.1915 in Rome; it is one of ma[ny] promotional posters f[or] operatic productions made in Italy at this time. **£600–800**

The performing arts have inspired posters of enormous visual appeal that also provide a fascinating visual record of the various personalities and theatrical productions of the last century. From c.1880 onwards in France, and to a lesser extent elsewhere in Europe, posters for theatre, dance, circus and opera were produced in vast quantities. This trend has continued throughout the 20th century and even posters for quite recent productions can be collectable. Posters advertising the performing arts are widely available at a very varied range of prices. Although the subject matter has traditionally always been popular with buyers, there is still plenty of scope for new collectors to build up a fascinating collection of late 19th- and 20th-century examples by well-known artists, and still not spend a fortune.

The theatre has traditionally relied on posters as an essential way of informing the public of when and where new productions were being held. Before the second half of the 19th century they were printed using letterpress techniques, mainly in black and white, and contained few images. Colourful pictorial posters were produced as soon as lithographic printing techniques improved, providing a far more visually arresting method of advertising entertainment.

The vast majority of late 19th- and early 20th-century posters were produced in France for the popular theatres, music halls and cabaret spectaculars of the day. Many of the most famous poster artists of the day, including Chéret, Toulouse-Lautrec and Mucha, produced designs for the various forms of entertainment available. By far the most valuable examples are those by

◄ **G. K. Benda (Georges Kugelmann)**
Mistinguett was a leading Parisian cabaret artiste, and posters featuring her, such as this example made c.1913, are avidly collected. £1,000–1,500

▲ **Jules Chéret**
One of many theatrical posters by Chéret, this example from 1900 advertises a typical Parisian show. £800–1,200

Toulouse-Lautrec, which can fetch hundreds of thousands of pounds for important, rare examples. The vast majority however cost between £200 and £5,000. Other factors which can affect value include the usual criteria of good design and condition as well as the identity of the personality depicted. Posters featuring cult stars with an especially keen following, such as Josephine Baker, will command a premium. Among the stars who feature on posters are Yvette Gilbert and Mistinguett, famous singers ; Jane Avril, May Belford and May Milton, celebrated turn-of-the-century cabaret stars; Loïe Fuller, renowned for her erotic dance of veils; La Goulue, a music hall dancer immortalized by Lautrec; the actress Sarah Bernhardt, memorably depicted by Mucha; and later stars of the 1920s, 1930s and 1940s such as Alice Soulie, Bagheera and the clown Grock.

Posters were also made in vast quantities to advertise the most fashionable Parisian venues and productions. Jules Chéret, one of the most prolific designers of posters for the theatre, produced designs advertising theatrical extravaganzas at the Musée Grévin, the Hippodrome, Théâtre de la Tour Eiffel, Théâtre de l'Opéra, Casino de Paris and Alcazar d'Eté. Other famous venues included the Moulin Rouge, which featured in posters by numerous artists including Lautrec; the Folies Bergère, the Lido and more recently the Crazy Horse. Although the venue itself usually has little bearing on the value of a poster, the design must be as colourful and evocative of the mood of the times as possible. The best examples are imbued with all the *joie de vivre*, colour, movement and gaiety for which the theatrical spectacles of Paris were famed the world over.

MONTANA FRANK SHOWS

▲ Wild West shows
An early 20th-century poster advertising a popular Wild
West show, published in Milwaukee. Similar posters for
touring shows were also printed in Europe. **£400–600**

Theatrical posters by leading poster artists are
always in keen demand, and apart from the
French artists Chéret and Toulouse-Lautrec there
are an abundance of other illustrious names to look
out for. Alphonse Mucha's reputation as a poster
artist was largely founded on his designs to promote
the actress Sarah Bernhardt and his posters show
her in many of her most famous roles at the Théâtre
de la Renaissance, Paris. These include Médée,
Gismonda, Hamlet, *La Dame aux Camélias*, Salomé,
Lorenzaccio – a play by Alfred de Musset in which
the actress is shown dressed in the medieval costume
of a man – and *La Samaritaine*. All Mucha's posters
featuring Bernhardt are popular with collectors and
fetch high sums, but rarity coupled with decorative
appeal also adds to the desirability of certain designs.
Posters advertising *La Samaritaine* and *La Dame aux
Camélias* are worth nearly twice as much as the
smaller version of *Lorenzaccio*, which is more common, although the larger version is also rare.

Théophile Alexandre Steinlen, the Swiss-born
contemporary of Toulouse-Lautrec who worked

extensively in Paris, also designed posters for the
theatre. One striking example for a musical production entitled *La Rêve* reveals the influence of
Japanese woodcuts in the rich use of surface pattern
and flat areas of colour – a style that was particularly
appropriate since the production had an oriental
theme. In the 1930s Paul Colin also produced some
very sought-after posters for dancers, magicians,
plays and other theatrical events. These include
designs for the Russian dancer Serge Lifar (see
p108), a charitable evening at the Palais de Chaillot
entitled *La Nuit de Paris*, and a play entitled *La
Tendre Ennemie* by André-Paul Antoine. Colin's
designs often incorporate oddly juxtaposed images
that are probably inspired by his interest in collage –
a key influence on Cubist artists. Among the most
visually appealing and collectable posters are those
reflecting the influence of prevailing artistic styles,
such as Art Nouveau, Surrealism and Cubism.

In Italy numerous posters for grand operatic
productions were made from the late 19th century
and these too are keenly collected, especially if they

◀ **Théophile Alexandre Steinlen**
A highly decorative poster, reflecting the influence of Japanese woodcuts, designed in 1891 to advertise *La Rêve*. £250–350

▼ **Jacques Faria**
One of a variety of posters by this artist promoting circus acts; printed c.1900 in Paris. £100–200

◀ **Alphonse Mucha**
This quintessentially Art Nouveau design advertises Sarah Bernhardt in *La Samaritaine* and was printed in 1896 by Champenois. £600–800

mention a famous opera or opera house. The best Italian theatrical posters are characterized by lavish and stylish designs and rich colouring that encapsulates the glamour of turn-of-the-century productions. Marcello Dudovich designed numerous posters for operas in Italy, printed by Chappuis in Bologna. Among his designs are posters for *Fedora* in 1899, and for the Scala company's tour at the Berlin Opera. Adolfo Hohenstein also designed opera posters, including one for Puccini's *La Bohème* published in 1895.

More recently collectable opera posters include designs made by David Hockney in the 1980s for the Metropolitan Opera, New York and Lyric Opera of Chicago. The most collectable of Hockney's posters are three large, striking designs printed by the Petersburg Press: *Parade*, *Three Bill Parade* and *Igor Stravinsky*. Hockney's numerous smaller posters for the opera are inexpensive unless they are signed.

Posters produced in Paris and, to a lesser extent, elsewhere in Europe around the turn of the century also reflect the enormous variety of travelling pro-

ductions. The famous Wild West show of Buffalo Bill aroused great attention and posters for it were produced both in the United States and in Europe to promote the show's arrival. These and posters for other similar Wild West productions are also keenly collected. Circus posters are the focus of attention for some collectors. Some advertise the whole circus – posters for Barnum & Bailey are often seen; others show individual acts. Rather gruesome "freak acts" are especially popular with collectors. In Switzerland posters for the Circus Knie are popular and can fetch moderate prices, while Polish circus posters are particularly affordable. Few artists are well-known for their circus subjects, though one exception is Jacques Faria. This artist, active in turn-of-the-century Paris, produced some notable designs for attractions such as Lyria, a performing dog, Jupiter Trio, a flying bar act, and Miss Bertha and Hilario, featuring a daring trapeze artist. Faria's designs are typically colourful and detailed with the central figures surrounded by vignettes showing them in action.

Food & Drink Posters

Collecting posters advertising wine, spirits, soft drinks and foods of every description

▲ **Nover**
Absinthe Vichet, published c.1900 by L. Revon & Cie. This example, by the artist known as Nover, is of a decorative design incorporating many Art Nouveau elements and is in good condition. **£1,800–2,000**

Food and drink have provided subject matter for designers from the origins of poster-making in the mid-19th century to the present day. The earliest posters, produced in the 1860s and 1870s, were not particularly colourful or aesthetically memorable but in the decades that followed artists developed the potential of the poster as a medium for advertising. Many of the leading poster artists of the late 19th and early 20th centuries, such as Jules Chéret, Leonetto Cappiello and Alphonse Mucha, turned their hand to designing such advertisements, and the resulting images became increasingly attractive.

Nearly all the best surviving early food and drink posters were designed by French artists, and follow a fairly routine format. Most examples show an attractive, often scantily clad, female figure in a dramatic pose

displaying the product. The figure is usually the most dominant part of the design while the lettering and the product itself play little part in the visual impact of the poster.

Most collectors of advertising posters for food and drink either concentrate on a particular item or are primarily interested in the artist concerned. Certain products have a keen following. Posters advertising absinthe are particularly popular, because the liqueur was the subject of so many paintings by artists of the late 19th and early 20th centuries, such as Manet and Toulouse-Lautrec.

During the 1900s food and drink posters of great style and decorative appeal began to be produced in other European centres. In Belgium Privat Livemont tailored his archetypal Art Nouveau imagery – a stylized woman set against a floral background – to promote biscuits, chocolate, tea and various

▼ **Bernard Villemot**
One of the most successful post-war designers, Villemot invariably relied on strong colours and simple shapes for impact. This example for the soft drink Orangina is printed in two sheets and dates from c.1970. **£300–400**

drinks. In Great Britain, John Hassall, a designer of notable posters for Coleman's mustard and Nestlé's milk, set up a school of poster artists whose members included Will Owen, the designer of the *Ah Bisto!* poster. Switzerland, Germany and Italy also produced interesting posters from this date onwards. However, perhaps because the French have always collected and admired poster art, examples from France are much more numerous than those that survive from other countries.

As the new streamlined Art Deco style took hold in the 1920s, designs became simpler yet more dramatic in their impact, with the lettering gaining importance overall. Adolphe Cassandre was one of the most outstanding exponents of this new style of poster.

Food and drink posters of the later 20th century are also highly collectable if they are visually striking, particularly if designed by a famous artist. Among the most renowned post-war designers of food and drink posters are the French artists Bernard Villemot, who created several advertisements for Orangina, and Raymond Savignac.

The artist, the image and the rarity of the design all play an important part in deciding a poster's value, although many highly decorative posters are still very affordable. Many early French posters for wines and spirits are decorative in style but are unsigned, and it is therefore impossible to identify the artist with certainty. Large posters are the most desirable; smaller sizes tend to be less sought after as they lack the same visual impact. The collector should keep in mind that poor condition can dramatically reduce the value of a poster unless the design is particularly rare and the artist is sought after.

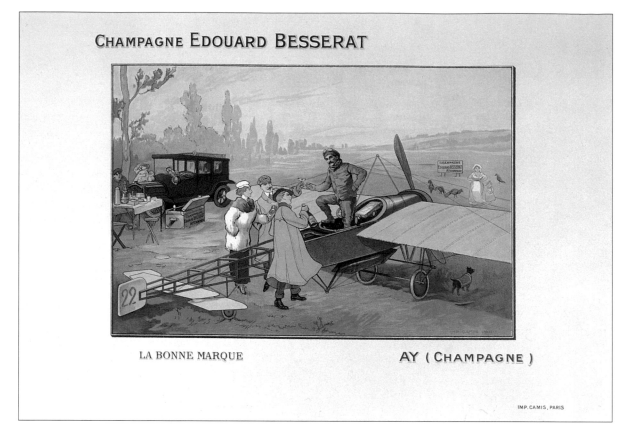

CHAMPAGNE EDOUARD BESSERAT

LA BONNE MARQUE

AY (CHAMPAGNE)

IMP. CAMIS, PARIS

▲ **Anonymous French artist**
The use of an aeroplane to promote a brand of champagne
makes this poster, printed c.1914, especially interesing. **£300–500**

A fascinating assortment of foods and drinks appears in French posters of the late 19th and early 20th centuries. Posters for drinks greatly outnumber those for foods and the product itself can often have a significant bearing on the value of the poster. In general posters for wines and liqueurs tend to be far more sought after than those for beer. The period charm of earlier (pre-1930s) posters makes them often more interesting and therefore more valuable than later examples. Early posters also often provide fascinating insights into the fashionable drinks, foods, costumes and social conventions of their time.

Some drinks were advertised for their medicinal properties as well as their delicious taste. Judging by the numerous posters designed by Jules Chéret, Leonetto Cappiello, Pal (Jean de Paléologue), L. Vallet, Misti (Ferdinand Mifliez) and others for Quinquina, it must have been one of the most popular drinks at the turn of the century. This fortified wine, made by several different companies including Dubonnet, was advertised not only as a tasty aperitif but also as a health-enhancing tonic. Rather

unexpectedly it contained quinine, an extract from the bark of the cinchona tree, more usually used as a remedy to treat fevers.

Another interesting drink that appears on early French posters is Kola or Kola Coca, the forerunner of the present-day Coca Cola. Like Quinquina, Kola was promoted as having miraculous medicinal properties as well as an appetizing taste. The appeal of posters for cola drinks has continued to endure and among the more recently collectable posters for food and drink are those designed in the 1950s, 1960s and 1970s for the Coca Cola company by the Swiss designer Herbert Leupin. Leupin also designed posters advertising mineral water, soap and winter sports.

Posters for champagne and sparkling wines are always in high demand and were produced extensively in both France and Italy. Eye-catching champagne posters include one by Leonetto Cappiello, designed for Champagne de Rochegre published in 1902, and an Italian example by Leopoldo Metlicovitz in the Art Nouveau style for Elba Champagne.

▼ **Misti (Ferdinand Mifliez)**
An advertisement for a fashionable aperitif, printed c.1900.
Quinquina was made by numerous manufacturers and appears
on many turn-of-the-century posters. **£500–700**

▲ **Leonetto Cappiello**
A colourful poster
advertising pâté de foie
gras, dating from c.1925.
Cappiello was one of the
most prolific of French
poster designers from
1900–40. **£500–700**

◄ **Marcello Dudovich**
A stunning turn-of-the-
century Italian poster
advertising Campari.
The racing vignette in
the background adds to
the obvious appeal of
the glamorous subject.
£500–700

Champagne's exclusive and glamorous image sometimes inspired artists to promote it in rather original
ways. The poster illustrated (facing page) shows
Champagne Edouard Besserat being sipped by a
pilot who has landed his fragile plane in a field close
to a fashionable picnic – by implication the exclusivity of air travel is associated with the exclusivity of
the champagne. This poster is anonymous and
therefore relatively modestly priced but examples
by known artists are far more valuable.

Elegance and exclusivity are frequently emphasized in Italian posters for food and drink, and
although they are far less numerous than those produced in France at the same time they are worth
looking out for as they are often extremely attractive. A typically striking example is the
turn-of-the-century poster designed by Marcello
Dudovich, which shows an elegant lady in her carriage at the races holding a diminutive glass of
Campari – ostensibly the subject of the poster.

As with any poster the identity of the artist is
also of prime importance in establishing the value of
food and drink posters. Among the most sought-

after and valuable posters for foods are those
designed by the Czechoslovak artist Alphonse
Mucha for biscuits and chocolate. Mucha is best
known for his posters advertising the plays of the
actress Sarah Bernhardt and many of his posters for
brands of food feature elegantly stylised female figures that closely resemble his depictions of
Bernhardt. One of his best-known commissions is a
calendar for Mexican & Masson chocolate, known as
The Four Ages of Man. Published in 1897 this series
of four posters shows figures in stylized landscapes
framed with typically elaborate borders.

Perhaps the most prolific French designer of
food and drink posters in the early decades of the
20th century was Leonetto Cappiello who designed
posters for various brands of cognac, champagne,
Quinquina, wines, absinthe, cordial, vermouth,
Campari and various mineral waters as well as several different types of food. Cappiello's most prized
and valuable posters are those which reflect his earlier style and the influence of Toulouse-Lautrec.
Later posters from the 1920s are usually less distinctive in style and tend to be far less valuable.

Film &
Entertainment

Posters in the newly collectable fields of rock, pop, psychedelia and cinema

In common with all other forms of poster, those for concerts and films were not designed to last. Once their usefulness was at an end, most were discarded. Thus, though some posters may originally have been produced in considerable quantities, their potential as collectable objects was seldom envisaged and few have survived, even for major films or musical events.

When evaluating entertainment posters, visual appeal of the design is often of secondary importance; it is the subject matter – the popularity of the film, band or musician featured on the poster, and the rarity of the object, on which price is primarily based. As with all posters, condition is also critical to value. While folding creases and pin holes are to be expected as part of the poster's life, any damage to the image itself will have a detrimental effect on value, and missing areas will reduce value even further.

In the early years of the film and pop music industry, posters provided the most effective way of promoting new bands or advertising new films. Early posters therefore chart the development of the film and rock and pop industries and provide a fascinating insight into the evolution of the entertainment industry as a whole.

The market for vintage film posters has traditionally been centred on the United States, having only relatively recently captured the imagination of British collectors. In general, American posters tend to command the highest prices. Posters are almost inseparable from the wealth of other film and rock and pop memorabilia that has recently surfaced as such a popular collecting area. For this reason, at auction entertainment posters have frequently appeared in sales of film or rock and pop memorabilia rather than in specialist poster auctions. However, sales dedicated to film or rock posters are becoming more common. The bulk of the collecting market is concentrated on posters made before the 1970s. Few posters less than 10 years old are collectable, although posters for cult movies are already becoming increasingly popular. Particular favourites with collectors are posters for Hitchcock films, those

◄ Tyrannosaurus Rex
An EMI promotional poster for the album *Tyrannosaurus Rex*, 1968. This was Marc Bolan's first album with the band (later known as T. Rex) and therefore especially sought after. **£200–300**

► Tom Wilkes
A poster advertising the Monterey International Pop Festival, 1967. Monterey was the first of the large festivals that became a feature of the pop scene. The metallic finish is a feature of many psychedelic posters. **£800–1,200**

▼ Martin Sharp
A poster for Bob Dylan's *Mr Tambourine Man*, 1967, incorporating a metallic finish. The use of concealed messages within the design is a feature of many psychedelic posters. **£200–500**

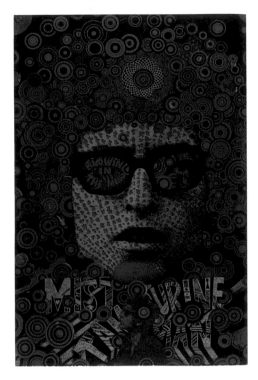

featuring James Bond, the *Star Wars* trilogy and for super-hero films such as the *Batman*, *Superman* and *Indiana Jones* series.

Film posters vary in size depending on their country of manufacture. In Britain the standard size is 40 x 30in/100 x 76cm, known as British Quad, whilst in America a regular format is known as the one sheet and measures 28 x 42in/70 x 107cm; there are also two and three sheet sizes. Billboard format sizes are much rarer than smaller ones but not necessarily more valuable as they are obviously more difficult to display.

Rock and pop posters fall into two main categories. The most desirable tend to be concert posters. These, by their very nature, were designed for display for only a short period and in a limited area and tend to have survived in very small numbers. Promotional posters for records usually incorporated the design of the album cover and were intended to be displayed in record shops. These may be generally less valuable but are often visually more interesting because they may reflect the work of leading artists of the day. Peter Blake

designed the sleeve for the Beatles' famous *Sergeant Pepper* album and the design of the inner sleeve was used for the promotional posters. Among the most influential designers of album covers were Roger Dean and Hipgnosis, a company responsible for many of the most original designs for album covers and promotional posters in the late 1960s and through the 1970s.

Fakes of film posters are rare, though honest reproductions of some popular posters have been made. These are usually identifiable by printing information that should make it clear they are reproductions. In the case of film posters this information will include the country of origin, the name of the studio and a serial number (usually incorporating the last two numbers of the year). Easily discernible reproductions of some rock posters have also been produced; fakes have appeared from time to time but have usually been quickly recognized. The paper and printing techniques are normally tell-tale signs and the market grapevine is an efficient method of passing on information of this nature.

►**Humphrey Bogart & Katharine Hepburn**

This poster for *The African Queen*, issued in 1951, is desirable because it features one of the great screen partnerships of the day, with typical emphasis on the action-packed and dramatic story line. £400–600

◄ **Charlie Chaplin**

Chaplin was one of the most sought-after of all film stars of the 1920s and posters of his landmark films such this example advertising *The Kid*, published in 1921 by First National US, are rare and command premium prices. £10,000–15,000

Film

From the earliest days of film-making, posters played a fundamental part in the promotion of new productions. Before radio and television, posters were the studio's only available method of informing an audience that a new film had been released. The poster's role was therefore to draw the eye, communicate the essence of the film, emphasize its title and glamorize the stars it featured.

The early history of films is dominated by the United States, and as a result American designers pioneered the use of images that were straightforward, if rather formulaic. Typical 1920s posters featured artists' portraits of the actors set against a particularly dramatic painted scene that encapsulated the content of the film. Because the concept of the star was still in its infancy, only a handful of names such as Charlie Chaplin, Mary Pickford, Douglas Fairbanks, Rudolph Valentino and Gloria Swanson had as yet achieved significant fame. In many early poster designs the name of the star was therefore accorded relatively little weight, the action and film title providing the central focus. Colour

was dramatically used – even though the films they advertised were in black and white! Throughout the 1920s, output was in relatively limited quantities but used high-quality production techniques. Interestingly, in these early days there was little overall control or uniformity to poster design because the film studios had yet to establish their international promotional networks. American films released in Britain were thus often promoted only by posters produced by individual cinemas.

For almost two decades the American film industry led the world but as Britain and other European countries gradually began to establish their own film industries, posters were produced to promote their own films. In Europe, the film industry used the established tradition of advertising by commissioning leading artists and illustrators, many of whom were influenced by various artistic movements of the day. Some of the most interesting designers include Paul Colin, who designed posters for French films including *Le Voyage Imaginaire*; Ronald Searle, the cartoonist and illustrator who

▲Mae West
Scene cards are among
a range of less expensive
promotional material issued
by the film companies. This
example from *I'm No Angel*,
1933, embodies the
sensuous charms of
its star. **£250–400**

◄James Bond
Posters advertising film super-
heroes, such as this example
issued in 1971 for the successful
Bond film *Diamonds Are Forever*,
have an increasing following with
collectors and are among the
most recently collectable film
posters. **£200–300**

designed the posters for *The Belles Of St Trinian's* and *The Lavender Hill Mob*; and G. Olivetti who designed the poster for Fellini's *La Dolce Vita*.

As the industry developed on both sides of the Atlantic, the cult of the star blossomed, boosted by a burgeoning publicity machine and several specialist magazines. Posters reflected the shift in emphasis, by paying increasing attention to the portraits of the actors and actresses and writing their names large, while relegating the action to the background. The film poster's golden age coincides with the film industry's heyday of the 1930s, 1940s and 1950s. Since many collectors of vintage posters are attracted primarily by their nostalgic appeal, the value of posters of this period often mirrors the success of the film they advertise. Posters for films such as *Dr Zhivago*, *Gone With The Wind*, *Casablanca*, *Psycho* and *The Wizard Of Oz* are avidly collected and prices for those in good condition remain predictably high. Also popular are posters featuring the great partnerships of Hollywood: Astaire and Rogers, Bogart and Bacall, Gable and Leigh.

Leading American poster designers include Saul Bass, who was responsible for many of the designs advertising Otto Preminger films, Hitchcock classics such as *Psycho*, *North By North West* and *Vertigo*; and Martin Scorsese films such as *Goodfellas* and *The Age Of Innocence*. Other leading American artists include Tom Chantrell, who designed posters for Twentieth Century Fox in the 1940s and 1950s, and Albert Hirschfeld, a prolific poster designer for M.G.M. Among the more affordably priced types of promotional film material are lobby cards or front of house stills. These were issued in sets of six or eight showing scenes from the film and were intended to provide audiences with a further inkling of what to expect from the film they were about to see. American examples are usually about 14 x 11in/35.5 x 28cm in size. Early lobby cards were designed by artists or featured photographic stills that were hand-coloured to make them more enticing. Lobby cards from the 1920s are rare and keenly collected but in general they tend to be less expensive than posters of the same film.

◄ The Beatles
An extremely rare hand-painted poster for the Beatles' appearance at the Kaiserkeller, Hamburg, 1960. The band played around 58 times on their first trip to Hamburg. This is the earliest known Beatles poster and sold for a record price of **£17,480** in 1996.

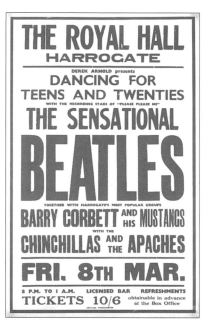

◄ **Early Beatles**
A poster for a concert in Harrogate in 1963. By this time Beatlemania was on the increase and the band are billed as the leading act. The poster is of a simple design by a local printer and has survived in excellent condition. **£3,000–3,500**

Rock & Pop

Until the mid-1960s, posters for rock and roll concerts were little more than functional statements whose job was simply to inform the public when and where an event would take place. Designs were typically rather unimaginative, comprised mainly of lettering, with little if any pictorial content, and were usually produced together with handbills which incorporated a ticket order form. In these early days of rock and roll, the money available to spend on the promotion of individual acts was limited, so posters were produced as cheaply as possible. If an artist was touring a chain of cinemas, for example, the poster design for each venue would be identical with just the venue's name differing. The posters would then have been displayed in the foyer of the cinemas and civic ballrooms involved.

Despite their limited visual appeal, posters of the 1950s and early 1960s can be keenly sought after, but only if the star whose performance they advertise has a high status with collectors. Values depend entirely on the reputation of the star; in the hierarchy of rock and roll memorabilia, posters for certain artists are far more desirable than equally rare examples of the same date for those with a less active following. Posters advertising events in the early careers of important stars are in particular demand because fewer tend to have survived than for those marking key concerts later in their careers.

Among British stars the Beatles occupy a unique position. All Beatles posters are collectable, early ones particularly so. The earliest known poster dates from October 1960 for a concert at the Kaiserkeller in Hamburg (see above) held only weeks after the band had settled on their name. This is one of a few produced for the club and when one appeared on the market recently it fetched over £17,000 – a world record price. Posters from concerts held in Liverpool clubs during 1961–62 are also very rare and even those dating from 1963 (when the band became nationally famous after constantly touring in the UK) are extremely scarce. Early posters used simple graphics usually showing the Beatles as support acts for other artists such as Roy Orbison, Gerry and the Pacemakers or Helen Shapiro.

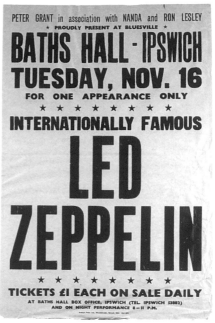

A poster for a concert at the Washington Hilton, 1968. The colourful image uses blue and flourescent orange inks on a yellow background. **£1,500–2,000**

▲ **Led Zeppelin**
An example of a simply designed early poster printed locally for the band's concert in Ipswich in November, 1970. **£1,500–2,000**

Posters for overseas concerts are also popular with collectors and can fetch extremely high sums. Beatles concert posters stopped when the group ceased touring in 1966, although posters were still produced to promote albums and films. Among the less expensive but more visually appealing Beatles posters are those sold in the Apple shop in London in the late 1960s. Designed by the Fool, a Dutch group whose work reflects the fashion for psychedelia, these were printed in large numbers and sold as decorative rather than promotional items.

Rock posters of the 1970s, 1980s and 1990s, although colourful, are far less visually interesting than those of the psychedelic era, and once again value depends on the following of the particular artist. The Rolling Stones, Jimi Hendrix and Led Zeppelin have a large body of collectors and therefore posters tend to fetch high sums; other slightly less valuable, though still collectable posters include those for Cream, Bob Dylan and Eric Clapton.

The Punk era of 1976–77 inspired some of the most innovative and controversial posters of recent decades. Stark images were designed by Jamie Reid in the "ransom note" style of graphics – so called because the lettering imitates the effect of a collage made from different typefaces cut from a news paper – as on a ransom note. Posters of this period became increasingly detailed, frequently incorporating bizarre images and juxtapositions which reflect the unconventional ethos behind the Punk movement. By 1977–78 as the New Wave emerged in British music, punk rock waned in popularity, and the distinctive style of poster which had promoted it gave way to a more formulaic approach to design, relying mainly on a tried and tested formula of simple lettering and a photograph of the star. So what are likely to become the most sought-after posters of the future? Since present-day poster design generally lacks the creative ingenuity of psychedelia or punk posters, their potential as collectable items depends entirely on the reputation of the star they promote – it seems probable that posters for successful stars rather than successful designs will continue to take precedence.

▼ **Mouse Studios**
Poster advertising a Grateful Dead concert at the Avalon
Ballroom, San Francisco, September 1966. **£300–400**

▼ **Mouse Studios**
Poster advertising a Grateful Dead concert at the Avalon
Ballroom, San Francisco, September 1966. **£300–400**

▶ **Martin Sharp**
Promotional poster for Jimi Hendrix, 1968. The typically
striking design makes brilliant use of colour. **£150–250**

Psychedelia

The psychedelic movement of the mid 1960s spawned a renaissance in the art of poster design in the United States and Britain, giving rise to some of the most visually arresting and innovative of all posters produced in the second half of the 20th century. With their swirling colours, amorphous shapes and bizarre lettering, psychedelic posters provide a potent reminder of the cultural movement that flourished on the west coast of America between 1965–1970. Flower power, free love, the hippie lifestyle and experimentation with mind-altering drugs, such as LSD, all played a part in the development of this short-lived artistic style. Posters emerged as psychedelia's most striking art form and provide fascinating time capsules recording this blossoming of artistic talent.

Psychedelic posters made their first appearance in the United States in the mid 1960s, when a handful of artists began to produce posters to promote forthcoming concerts. Their designs incorporated a far more pictorial and vibrantly colourful approach to poster design. Lettering was often extraordinarily stylized and difficult to decipher requiring an understanding of the style itself in order to be read. The best-known American exponents of psychedelic posters include Stanley Mouse, Peter Max and Rick Griffin. Much of their work was commissioned by Bill Graham, a promoter and owner of several famous venues on both coasts of the United States. Posters were made both to promote concerts of American artists such as Jefferson Airplane, Jimi Hendrix and the Grateful Dead, as well as those visiting from Britain.

Posters were intended to be used for a short period of time and only within a relatively small area, so print runs were strictly limited in numbers. Perhaps strangely, considering their short intended lifespan, the enduring artistic merit of these vibrant images also lies in the fact that they employed many of the most innovative and expensive printing techniques available at the time. Silkscreen techniques – which are time-consuming and labour-intensive –

► **Michael English and Nigel Weymouth (Hapshash and The Coloured Coat)**
A silkscreen poster advertising a concert by Pink Floyd at the UFO Club in London in July, 1967.
£400–500

▼ **Rick Griffin**
A poster designed to promote a Quicksilver Messenger Service concert at the Avalon Ballroom, January 1968. £100–150

◄ **Wes Wilson**
A poster advertising a concert by Buffalo Springfield and the Steve Miller Blues Band at the Fillmore Auditorium, San Francisco, April 1967.
£50–80

were often used; designs were packed with newly available fluorescent colours and metallic finishes; and the paper is often of the best quality.

Interest in psychedelic posters developed quickly and many of Graham's posters were reprinted for purely decorative purposes, not long after their first publication. Interest has continued to grow in the last decade and exhaustive research on the subject has been carried out in America. All Graham's posters have been catalogued and numbered, and each design is listed with its number – known as the BG series. Reprints are identifiable from a suffix number. Rarity and decorative appeal are fundamental in establishing the value of most posters, unless they are for a particularly sought-after artist such as Hendrix, in which case the name alone commands a premium. Reprints are worth a fraction of the price of those from the first printing.

The other major strand in the development of psychedelic posters took place in Britain, where the American-led fashion also quickly spread to British designers of concert posters. Leading European names include Hapshash and The Coloured Coat formed by Nigel Weymouth and Michael English; and the Fool – a design team of three Dutch artists who designed posters for the Beatles.

In general British psychedelic posters are less thoroughly documented than American ones. Like their American counterparts, British posters were made using the best printing techniques and in limited numbers and are probably even rarer than American examples today. Prices have risen dramatically in recent years, fuelled by the general increase in interest in rock and roll memorabilia; but British posters still tend to lag behind American ones in terms of value.

The golden age of the psychedelic poster waned at the end of the 1960s. As the rock industry grew and huge world tours became the norm, cheap posters with elements of photomontage replaced them as a far less costly method of promoting a band – but a far less interesting one artistically.

Framing & Displaying Prints & Posters

A frame's function is both to enhance and protect the print within it; acting as a magnet to the eye by attracting attention to the image.

No matter how beautiful a print or striking a poster, if it is poorly displayed you will considerably diminish its impact. However, both at auction and in dealer's galleries a large proportion of the prints and posters on offer are sold unframed, and it is worth taking some time to choose a frame carefully.

Framing traditions

Many prints and posters nowadays considered worthy of framing and hanging on a wall were not originally intended to be displayed in this way at all. Until the end of the 17th century prints were nearly always pasted in volumes and kept in the connoisseur's library; large sheets were usually folded to fit the albums in which they were stored. Posters, on the other hand, were cheaply printed on large sheets of paper – made to be thrown away as soon as their purpose had been served. As the 17th century progressed, prints became increasingly appreciated as works of art in their own right, and collectors began framing their collections of mezzotint portraits or landscape etchings and displaying them as a way of making known their good taste and learning.

Print rooms

By the 18th century prints were often sold framed and glazed or ready to be pasted directly onto walls to create the fashionable print rooms of the day. The fashion for print rooms originated in Paris in the early 18th century, gradually taking hold in Britain and Ireland by the mid-century. Both professional and amateur collectors enjoyed creating print rooms and specially printed borders were produced to frame the images, which in Britain were usually pasted onto brightly coloured walls.

Styles of frames

Throughout the 18th century glass was expensive and only available in relatively small panes hence most prints were framed without mounts, with their margins trimmed virtually to the image. Stipple engravings of genre subjects (see p52) are often found in their old *verre églomisé* (painted glass) frames in black and gold and some have wonderfully elaborate carved and gilded frames. The Hogarth frame, a plain ebonized moulded frame sometimes edged in a narrow gilded border, became popular in the 19th century for horizontal narrative and landscape prints. The frame was named after the frame-making family of the same name, but because it was so often used to frame the artist William Hogarth's famous series of prints, it has become largely associated with the artist rather than the company of framers where it originated.

Buying framed prints

Prints in their original frames are usually far more desirable than those in replacement frames and unless the frame is badly damaged you should think carefully before discarding it. In recent years the growing popularity of stipple engravings has led to a rise in prices for those in *verre églomisé* frames, and where possible these should be repaired as they can add greatly to a print's value. Many prints bought in their original frames will show evidence of discolouration, however, caused by the use of acidic backboards or mounts (see p148). This problem should be properly rectified while preserving the original frame.

Mounts

Mounts prevent the print from touching the glass and draw attention to the delicacy of the image. Although mounts were not generally used for framing prints until the 19th century, today pale mounts in cream or buff to harmonize with the colour of the paper are often used, especially for

◀ *Verre églomisé*
This classical muse was engraved after Giovanni Battista Cipriani by the leading stipple engraver Francesco Bartolozzi. It is typically displayed in an early 19th-century *verre églomisé* frame. Stipple engravings in this type of frame are highly collectable.
£100–150

▶ Decorative frames

A Heroic Irish Volunteer,
a stipple engraving after Henry
Singleton by Delatre. The early
19th-century frame reflects the fashion
for naval motifs and greatly enhances the
decorative appeal of the subject. **£200–300**

decorative subjects and botanical and scientific prints. Mounts are usually slightly wider at the base than the top. If the base of the mount is the same width as the top, the print can look as if it is falling out of the bottom of its frame, once it is hung.

Choosing modern frames

Although buying new frames is largely a matter of personal choice, there are a few general guidelines that are worth bearing in mind. A frame should enhance the print rather than overwhelm it. Therefore, even if you want to emphasize a print, it is better to use a wider mount rather than choose a frame that is too powerful and heavy. One of the most popular ways of adding visual interest to a wide mount is by the addition of wash lines, which draw the eye into the image and break up an otherwise plain surface. Wash lines may be monochrome or tinted to provide a link with the colours in the print. Gold lines are also often used on mounts in gilded frames. Prints that are hung in groups look attractive if they are in frames that harmonize with one another, since this gives coherence to even the most eclectic collection. This does not mean that all the frames need to be identical, merely that if they are of similar weight or colour they will provide a visual link that can enhance the overall effect of the display.

Posters

Because of their large size posters are best displayed in plain, light-weight frames and should be glazed with perspex (plexiglas) rather than glass. Perspex is not only much lighter in weight but also less dangerous in the event of an accident because it does not shatter. The fragility of the paper used for most posters means that they usually need some form of support before framing. Linen or japan paper are both acceptable forms of support and will not generally detract from their value, provided they have been mounted using vegetable paste, which is reversible. (For further details on care and restoration see p148).

Conservation & Restoration

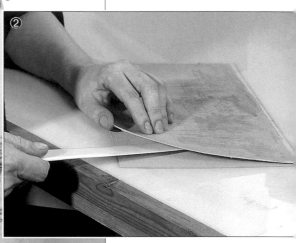

❶ Carefully washing a print in a bath of water to remove stains caused by foxing.

❷ An old acidic backing, which has been soaked to soften the glue, is gently removed from a print.

❸ The remaining pieces of glue and backing are removed by applying steam.

The terms "conservation" and "restoration" are often considered interchangeable and are used rather loosely. To the professionals, however, the general consensus is that "conservation" means the making safe of a print, stabilizing any damage that may have occurred and preserving it from further deterioration. This might mean gently cleaning stains, stabilizing flaking or cracking pigment, mending tears, replacing lost areas of paper in a way that is not deceptive to future generations and, if necessary, remounting with acid-free mounts. "Restoration" means returning the print to its original state and usually involves more extensive cleaning and repainting. With a restored work the aim is often to disguise the signs of age or damage.

How much restoration does it need?

If you have recently bought an old print you may wonder how much, if any, restoration it requires. The modern day approach to care and restoration has changed considerably in recent decades. The trend is towards as little restoration as possible. In other words a print should be allowed to age gracefully without deterioration impairing your enjoyment of it. So if the paper seems slightly yellow in tone you may justifiably feel this is all part of its charm and keep it carefully enough to preserve its present state without any dramatic restoration at all. If, on the other hand the print is excessively dirty or covered with foxing stains it may benefit from gentle cleaning.

Choosing a restorer

Always use professional restorers. Restoration is a highly skilled art; an unqualified restorer can cause untold damage and greatly reduce the value of antique prints – most sales at auction contain at least one disastrous result of poor restoration. You can find a local qualified restorer through one of the various trade associations such as the Conservation Unit, the Fine Art Guild, the Association of British Picture Restorers, the United Kingdom Institute of Conservation, or The Institute of Paper Conservation (see p152 for addresses). Restorers registered with one of these organizations are professionally qualified and will advise you on the necessary conservation and restoration as well as help you to care for your print correctly once you have taken it home.

Causes of damage

Paper is made from absorbent fibres and will react with the air surrounding it, as well as anything that comes into direct contact with its surface. Early prints on handmade linen fibre paper made from good-quality fibres are often less vulnerable to damage than those on cheaper paper made from the 19th century onwards. Later paper often incorporated wood pulp which contained inherent impurities, such as lignin, an acidic substance. Over a period of time such impurities cause the deterioration and eventual disintegration of the paper. Many old prints (even those on good-quality handmade paper) may at some stage have been stuck down onto an acidic backboard or mounted on acidic card. These too will cause stains and discolouration where they come in contact with the paper. A professional restorer will usually be able to remove acidic discolouration and stabilize the deterioration.

Adhesive tapes are also often found attaching old prints to their backboards and these can cause serious staining. Prints that have been kept in a damp atmosphere are often discoloured with small circular brown marks known as "foxing". This is caused by a type of mould that grows in damp atmospheres. Paper made from wood pulp is particularly susceptible to foxing stains. Excessive dampness may also cause paper to become misshapen and wrinkled. Stains and damage caused by adhesive tape, foxing or damp can usually be dealt with highly effectively by professional restorers.

Methods of restoration

The first stage in this process is usually to wash the print carefully in a bath of plain water. Remaining stains are then gently removed with the use of chemical agents. Damage from insect attack is usually identifiable on the surface of prints as areas in which the paper is thin and the surface uneven or by small holes. Insects are often attracted by the size (glue) used to seal the paper and if still active they can also be dealt with by chemical treatment.

Caring for prints

Prints should be protected from three main causes of deterioration: pollution, sunlight and damp. Pollutants in the atmosphere can be absorbed by the porous fibres that make up paper causing damaging discolouration. To avoid this prints should be entirely sealed within their frames and backing. In the 19th century many prints were backed with poor-quality wood which has often split and allowed air to penetrate to the paper. This causes air burns on the back of the paper, visible as a brown stripe of staining which eventually shows through to the front of the work of art.

Light causes the fading of coloured pigments and the discolouration of the paper itself. While damage caused by pollution can usually be helped by professional restoration, damage caused by fading is irreparable, so the most important rule in caring for prints, especially those with colouring, is to protect them from sunlight.

A damp atmosphere can also be dangerous and the small brown spots commonly seen on prints, known as foxing, are a type of mould that flourishes in a damp atmosphere. Foxing stains can usually be removed by restorers, but can be avoided by storing prints in dry conditions.

Mounts

Mounts should be made from conservation or museum board, which are acid free and will prevent further damage caused by acidity. The mount should be made from two pieces of card and the picture should be secured with hinges at the top edge to the back mount. Do not glue the picture to the backing card – this can cause the paper to split and may necessitate later repairs. The mount should be thick enough to prevent the surface of the paper from coming into contact with the glass. The backboard should be made from acid-free cardboard or tempered hard board and sealed with good-quality tape to prevent air from penetrating.

Posters

Posters may be mounted onto japan paper or a linen backing using a water soluble vegetable based paste and hinge mounted with acid-free tape or tacked onto an acid-free backboard. Household adhesive tape can cause serious damage and is not suitable for attaching posters to their mounts. Posters (and prints) should never be dry mounted (bonded to adhesive-treated backing paper using heat) since this is an irreversible process that greatly reduces their value. Tears may be repaired using acid-free tape. As with other forms of prints the inks used in posters are susceptible to fading and posters therefore need to be displayed away from direct sunlight.

Paper

Examining the paper on which an image is printed is one of the most reliable ways of dating and authenticating it. Paper is believed to have been invented in China in 200AD, although in Europe it was not made until c.1100. Until the invention of the paper machine in the late 18th century in France, all paper was made by hand from cotton and linen rags that were soaked, boiled and beaten to form a fibrous pulp.

Laid paper

Laid paper was commonly used for prints made before c.1800. It was made by putting a wire grid into the fibrous pulp so that a sediment of fibres was deposited evenly over the surface. The paper was then unmoulded, pressed between felt blankets, dried and then covered with a gelatin or starch size to seal the surface and make it less absorbent. Laid paper is recognizable by its uneven surface and the visible grid of lines running through the fibres that were made by the wires of the sieve. Thin "laid" lines run vertically parallel to one another and are intersected at intervals by broader horizontal "chain lines".

Wove paper

The problems posed by the rough uneven surface of laid paper were overcome with the 18th-century development of wove paper. Wove paper was popularized in the 1780s by James Whatman, one of the most famous British paper manufacturers. The paper was made using a sieve with a finer mesh than that used for the laid method. The result had no visible lines, providing a much smoother surface on which to print.

Wood pulp paper

During the Industrial Revolution the increasing demand for paper led to the mechanization of papermaking. Wood pulp was used as a cheaper alternative to rags; the resulting paper tended to be brittle and to discolour because impurities in wood pulp (lignin) tended to cause acidic staining and to break down the fibres. Most posters were printed on wood pulp paper.

Watermarks

Watermarks are formed by wires held into the papermaking mould, and are commonly incorporated into paper as a manufacturer's mark. They are usually visible if a sheet of paper is held to the light and can help in dating a watercolour and in identifying its place of origin (there are several dictionaries of marks). Do not assume that the date of work is the same as that of the paper, since stocks of paper were often kept for several years before use.

Modern paper

Hand-papermaking methods are still occasionally used for expensive types of watercolour paper, and pulped linen and rags are used for quality art paper.

Sizes

Paper is traditionally cut into standard sizes:
Foolscap 13¼ x 16½in (34 x 42cm)
Crown 15 x 20in (38 x 50cm)
Large Post 16½ x 20in (42 x 50cm)
Printing Demy 17½ x 22½in (44 x 57cm)
Printing Medium 18 x 23in (45 x 58cm)
Royal 20 x 25in (50 x 64cm)
Imperial 30 x 22in (76 x 56cm)
Atlas 34 x 26in (86 x 66cm)

Standard poster sizes

Sizes vary according to the poster's subject, intended purpose and country of origin. The following dimensions are for the most commonly seen standard sized posters. Discrepancies in size may mean that an image has been trimmed and can, in some cases, may indicate a reproduction.
English sizes
40 x 50in (102 x 127cm) (Quad Royal)
40 x 30in (102 x75cm)
40 x 25in (102 x 64cm) (Double Royal)
Swiss 50 x 35in (127 x 90cm)
French 49 x 35in (125 x 89cm)
63 x 47 (160 x 120cm)
General travel sizes
40 x 30in (102 x 75cm)

What to Read

Arts Council of Great Britain, *British Sporting Painting 1650–1850* (1974)

Ball, A. and Martin, M., *Price Guide to Baxter Prints* (1974)

Bargiel, Rejande and Zagrodzki C., *Steinlen Affichiste* (1986)

Barnicoat, John, *Posters: A Concise History* (1972)

Bazin, Jean-François, *Les Affiches de Villemot* (1985)

Bridson, G. D. R., *Plant and Animal Illustration* (1990)

Broido, Lucy, *The Posters of Jules Chéret* (1980)

Calloway, Stephen, *English prints for the Collector* (1980)

Castleman, Riva, *Prints of the 20th Century* (1976)

Chilvers, Ian and Osborn, Harold, *The Oxford Dictionary of Art* (1988)

Clarke, Michael, *The Tempting Prospect* (1981)

Desmond, Ray, *The Wonders of Creation* (1986)

Eichenberg, Fritz, *The Art of the Print* (1976)

Ford, B. J., *Images of Science* (1992)

Franciscono, Marcel, *The Modern Dutch Poster - The First Fifty Years* (1987)

Gascoigne, Bamber, *How to Identify Prints* (1986)

Godfrey, Richard, *Printmaking in Britain: A General History* (1978)

Goldman, Paul, *Looking at Prints, Drawings and Watercolours: A Guide to Technical Terms* (1988)

Goldman Sporting Life, British Museum (1983)

Griffiths, Antony, *Prints and Printmaking* (1980)

Haworth-Booth, Mark E., *McKnight Kauffer: A Designer and his Public* (1979)

Hillier, Bevis, *Posters* (1969)

Horn, Maurice, *The World Encyclopedia of Cartoons* (1980)

Horne, Alan, *The Dictionary of 20th-Century British Book Illustrators*

(1994)

Houfe, Simon, *Dictionary of British Book Illustrators 1800–1914* (new ed. 1994)

Labarre, E. J., *Dictionary and Encyclopedia of Paper and Papermaking* (1952)

Lambert, Susan, *The Image Multiplied* (1987)

Mackenzie, Ian, *British Prints* (1987)

Margadant, Bruno, *The Swiss Poster, 1900–1983* (1983)

Mayer, Ralph, *Collins Dictionary of Art Terms and Techniques* (1991)

Miller's Picture Price Guide (1995)

Mitzman, M. E., *George Baxter and the Baxter Prints* (1978)

Montry, Annie de and Lepeuve, Françoise, *Voyages, Les Affiches de*

Roger Broders (1991)

Moreland, Carl and Bannister, David *Antique Maps* (1983)

Mouron, Henri, *A. M. Cassandre* (1985)

Osborne, Harold (ed.), *The Oxford Companion to Art* (1970)

Rennert, Jack and Weill, Alain, *Alphonse Mucha: Toutes les Affiches et Panneaux* (1984)

Robinson, Andrew *Paper in Prints* (1977)

Bernstein, David *The Shell Poster Book* (1992)

Shikes, R. E., *The Art of Satire: Painters as Caricaturists* (1984)

Simpson, M. T. and Huntley, M., *Sotheby's Caring for Antiques* (1992)

Wilder, F. F., *English Sporting Prints* (1974)

Useful Addresses

MAJOR AUCTION HOUSES

Bearnes
Avenue Road, Torquay, Devon TQ2 5TG

Biddle & Webb
Ladywood Middleway, Birmingham B16 0PP

Bonhams
Montpelier Street, London SW7 1HH

Christie's
8 King Street, St James's, London SW1Y 6QT

Dreweatt & Neate
Donnington Priory, Donnington, Newbury, Berkshire RG13 2JE

Henry Spencer & Son
20 The Square, Retford, Nottinghamshire DN22 6BX

Lawrence's of Crewkerne
South Street, Crewkerne, Somerset TA18 8AB

Lots Road Auction Galleries
71 Lots Road, London SW10 0RN

Mallams
St Michael's Street, Oxford OX1 2EB

Outhwaite & Litherland
Kingsway Galleries, Fontenoy Street, Liverpool L3 2BE

Phillips
Blenstock House, 7 Blenheim Street, New Bond Street, London W1Y 0AS

Russel Balwin & Bright
Rylelands Road, Leominster, Herefordshire HR6 8NZ

Sotheby's
34–35 New Bond Street, London W1A 2AA

Woolley & Wallis
56–61 Castle Street, Salisbury, Wiltshire SP1 3SU

MAJOR ART AND ANTIQUES FAIRS

The London Original Print Fair
Royal Academy of Arts, Burlington House, London

West London Antiques Fair

Kensington Town Hall, Hornton Street, London

LAPADA Antiques and Fine Art Fair
National Exhibition Centre, Birmingham

Palais des Beaux-Arts
10 Rue Royal, Brussels, Belgium

Northern Antiques Fair
The Yorkshire Showground, Harrogate, N. Yorkshire

KAM Art and Antiques Fair of Switzerland
Messe Zurich

Fine Art and Antiques Fair
National Hall, Olympia, London

Chester Antiques Show
The County Grandstand, Chester Racecourse, Cheshire

Harrogate Antique and Fine Art Fair
The Royal Bath Assembly Rooms, Harrogate, N. Yorkshire

The Chelsea Antiques Fair
Chelsea Old Town Hall, King's Road, London

The Bath Decorative and Antiques Fair
The Pavilion, North Parade Road, Bath

The European Fine Art Fair
MECC, Maastricht, The Netherlands

British International Antiques Fair
National Exhibition Centre, Birmingham

Thames Valley Antiques Dealers' Association
School Hall, Eton College, Eton, Windsor, Berks

Buxton Antiques Fair
The Octagon, The Pavilion Gardens, Buxton, Derbyshire

BADA Fair
Duke of York's Headquarters, Chelsea, London

The Fine Art and Antiques Fair
Olympia, London

The Grosvenor House Art and Antiques Fair
Grosvenor House Hotel, Park Lane, London

South of England Showground
Ardingly, Sussex

Edinburgh Annual Antiques Fair
Edinburgh, Scotland

National Exhibition Centre August Fair
NEC, Birmingham

West London Antiques Fair
Kensington Town Hall, Hornton Street, London

LAPADA Antiques Fair
The Royal College of Art
Kensington Gore, London

Pan
The Park Hall, Amsterdam, The Netherlands

The Print Fair
The Park Avenue Armory, Park Ave. & 67th Street, New York

Westminster Antiques Fair
Royal Horticultural Hall, Vincent Square, London

ART AND ANTIQUES MARKETS AND CENTRES

Bath
Bath Antique Market
Guinea Lane, Lansdown Rd, Bath BA1 5NB (Wed)

Birmingham
Holliday Wharf Antiques Centre
164-166 Holliday Street, Birmingham B11 PJ

Derbyshire
Chappell's Antiques & Fine Arts Centre
King Street, Bakewell, Derbyshire DE45 1DZ

Hertfordshire
Herts & Essex Antiques Centre
The Maltings, Station Road, Sawbridgeworth, Herts CM21 9JX

London
Alfie's Antiques Market
13-25 Church Street, London NW8 8DT
(Tues–Sat)

Useful Addresses

Antiquarius
King's Road, London SW3 5ST
Bermondsey Market
Bermondsey St, London SE1 3UW
(Fri)
Camden Passage
Islington, London N1 8DU
(Wed & Sat)
Grays Antique Market
58 Davies Street, London W1Y 1LB
Portobello Road Market
Portobello Road
London W11 (Sat)
Lincolnshire
Hemswell Antiques Centres
Caenby Corner Estate, Hemswell Cliff,
Gainsborough, Lincs DN21 5JJ
Nottinghamshire
Portland Street Antiques Centre
27–31 Portland Street, Newark, Notts
NG24 4XF
Oxfordshire
The Swan at Tetsworth
High Street, Tetsworth, Oxon OX1 7AB
Sussex
Great Grooms Antiques Centre
Great Grooms, Billingshurst, West
Sussex
Somerset
Taunton Antiques Centre
27–29 Silver Street, Taunton, Somerset
TA1 3DH (Mon)
Worcester
Worcester Antiques Centre
Reindeer Court, Mealcheapen Street,
Worcester WR1 2DS

ANTIQUES AND FINE ART TRADE ASSOCIATIONS

The International Fine Print Dealers
Association, 485 Madison Avenue,
15th Floor, New York, NY 10022
The only international print dealers
organization, the Association
provides a directory of strictly vetted
dealers from around the world.
Dealers are elected to membership.
British Antique Dealers Association,
(BADA), 20 Rutland Gate, London SW7
1BD
London and Provincial Antique
Dealers Association (LAPADA),
Suite 214, 535 King's Road, London
SW10 0SZ
Society of London Art Dealers (SLAD)
91 Jermyn Street, London SW1Y 6JB
The Fine Art Trade Guild, 16–18
Empress Place, London SW6 1TT

RESTORATION ASSOCATIONS

The Institute of Paper Conservation
Leigh Lodge, Leigh, Worcester,
WR6 5LB
The Conservation Unit
Museums & Galleries Commission
16 Queen Anne's Gate
London SW1H 9AA
United Kingdom Institute of

Conservation (UKIC)
Whitehorse Mews
Westminster Bridge Road
London SE1 7QD
**Association of British Picture
Restorers**
Station Avenue, Kew, Surrey
TW9 3QA

SELECTED DEALERS

A selection of some of the many print
dealers; many operate from private
premises and you would be advised to
make contact before going to see
them. The trade associations listed will
also be able to provide a listing of print
dealers in your area.
Great Britain
Abbott and Holder
30 Museum Street, London WC1A 1LH
**Austin/Desmond Contemporary
Books**
68/69 Great Russell St, Pied Bull Yard,
London WC1B 3BN
Berkeley Square Gallery
23a Bruton St, London W1X 8JJ
Lucy Campbell
123 Kensington Church St, London
W8 7LP
Charnwood Antiques
P Moorhouse, Greystones, Coalville,
Leicester LE67 4RN
Gordon Cooke
112 Princes House, Kensington Park
Road, London W11 3BW
Alan Cristea Gallery
31 Cork St, London W1X 2NU
Andrew Edmunds
44 Lexington St, London W1R 3HL
The Fine Art Society
148 New Bond St, London W1Y 0JT
Flowers East
199–205 Richmond Rd, London E8
3NJ
Garton & Co
Roundway House, Devizes, Wiltshire
SN10 2EG
H. J. Gerrish
The Old Vicarage, Penrhos, Raglan,
Gwent, South Wales NP5 2LE
Graham and Oxley Ltd
73 Gloucester Terrace, London W2
3DH
Grosvenor Prints
28 Shelton St, London WC2H 9HP
Julian Hartnoll
14 Mason's Yard, Duke Street, St
James's, SW1Y 6BU
Elizabeth Harvey-Lee
1 West Cottages, Middle Aston Road,
North Aston, Oxfordshire, OX6 3QB
Lumley Cazalet Ltd
4 New Burlington St, London W1X 1FE
Christopher Mendez
58 Jermyn St, London SW1Y 6LP
Frederick Mulder
83 Belsize Park Gardens, London NW3
4NJ

Odyssey Fine Arts
Alvaro Dias, Tower Bridge Business
Complex, Clement's Road, London
SE16 4DG
The Parker Gallery
Brian J Newbury, 28 Pimlico Road,
London SW1W 8LJ
Michael Prevost
Long Melford Antiques Centre, Chapel
Maltings, Long Melford, Suffolk,
CO10 9HX
Frank T. Sabin
John Sabin, 13 The Royal Arcade, Old
Bond St, London W1X 3HD
O' Shea Gallery
120a Mount Street, London W1Y 5HB
G J Saville
Foster Clough, Hebden Bridge, West
Yorkshire HX7 5QZ
The Schuster Gallery
14 Maddox St, London W1R 9PL
Bernard J. Shapero
80 Holland Park Av, London W11 3RE
Trowbridge Gallery
555 King's Road, London SW6 2EB
William Weston Gallery
7 Royal Arcade, Albemarle St, London
W1X 4JN
Wiseman Originals
34 West Square, London, SE11 4SP
Europe
Galerie André Candillier
26 Rue de Seine, 75006 Paris, France.
Galerie K
Bjorn Farmannsgate 6
0271 Oslo, Norway
Graphic Studio Gallery
Through The Arch, Cope St, Dublin 2
J. Y. Lhomond Ltd
Stand 11 and 25, Marché Vernaison,
99 rue des Rosiers, 93400 St Ouen,
France
Kunsthandlung Helmut H. Rumbler
Borsenplatz 13–15, D 60313 Frankfurt,
Germany
USA
Dolan/Maxwell inc
2046 Rittenhouse Square, Philadelphia,
PA 19103-5021
Hill-Stone inc
Box 273 Gracie Station, New York, NY
10028
N.W. Lott
1771 Post Road East, Suite 271,
Westport, CT 06880
Paul McCarron & Susan Schulman
Graham Gallery Building, 1014 Madison
Avenue, New York, NY 10021
R. S. Johnson Fine Art
645 North Michigan Avenue
Chicago, IL 60611
Gerhard Wurzer Gallery
1217 South Shepherd Drive
Houston, TX 77019
**Marilyn Pink Master Prints &
Drawings/Fine Arts Ltd.**
P.O. Box 491446, 509 Avondale
Avenue, Los Angeles, CA 90049

GLOSSARY

Acid bath The container of acid into which a plate is immersed to etch it.

Acid free Used with reference to paper or board mounts. The term implies that the material has a neutral pH and is therefore resistant to foxing.

Acrylic Term for synthetic water-based paints first made in the 1930s that can be used as a substitute for oil paints.

After When used to describe a print the term implies the print is a copy of a known work by another artist.

Appliqué Design in which parts have been separately attached to the surface to form part of the image or pattern.

Aquatint Type of tonal etching simulating the effect of a watercolour (see p34).

Arabesque Curvilinear pattern made up from intertwining shapes.

Artist's book (*livre d'artiste*) A volume with illustrations designed by the artist and produced in small limited editions, usually with the artist's signature at the back.

Artist's proof or **AP** Prints made in addition to the the main edition and often signed as such by the artist. The number of artist's proofs varies with each edition but is usually no more than 10 per cent of the main edition.

Atelier An artist's studio or workshop.

A trois crayons Chalk drawing using black, white and sanguine chalk. Crayon manner prints emulating these drawings were made after Boucher and other artists.

Avant-garde Term used to describe art that is especially innovative.

Background Part of the composition that appears furthest away.

Bite The effect of acid on an etched plate.

Bitumen A tar-like substance sometimes used in addition to wax and other ingredients to form the acid-resistant ground used for etching.

Blister Area of paint in which the surface is lifting away from the support; blistering is often caused by excessive heat or damp.

Board Heavy, stiff, thick type of paper used as a support for a work of art.

Bodycolour Watercolour to which an opaque medium has been added, used for handcolouring on some types of print.

Bon à tirer or **BAT** Sometimes found written on a proof indicating it has been approved for editioning.

Burin Tool used by an engraver to draw lines on the metal plate; when used the burin cuts out a distinctive V-shaped segment from the plate.

Burnishing The process of smoothing and polishing a metal plate to produce a rich, smooth sheen.

Burr The residue thrown up by the pointed tool used to make a drypoint, giving a distinctive soft blurred line.

Capriccio Imaginary architectural scene; or a composition containing strange imaginary subjects.

Cartoon Originally a term used to describe a preparatory drawing for a work of art. Cartoons became associated with humorous drawings in the mid-19th century.

Catalogue raisonée A reference book in which all the known works by a particular artist are included. *Catalogues raisonées* are often invaluable in authenticating prints.

Chiaroscuro Depiction of contrasting light and shade.

Chiaroscuro woodcut Woodcut printed in tonal colour simulating a wash drawing.

Chromo or **Chromolithograph** Commercial type of colour-printed lithograph from the late 19th century.

Collagraph Print from a block applied with "found objects".

Collograph Print made from a photomechanical process, in which the design is drawn on plastic and directly exposed to a light sensitive plate.

Collector's marks Small stamps and marks usually comprising a monogram found on works of art showing they have been in an important collection.

Crayon manner engraving An 18th century intaglio technique used mainly in France in which the image is created from a series of soft lines using roulettes and needles to simulate the effect of a chalk drawing (see p26).

Cross hatching Shade and tone depicted in lines running at two or more different angles.

Cyma curve Continuous double curve used as a profile for moulding and on architectural motifs.

Daguerreotype Early photographic process invented by J. M. Daguerre in 1839.

Deckle edge Uneven edge on paper, showing it has not been mechanically cut; usually associated with paper of good heavy quality.

Découpage A decorative technique, similar to collage, involving the use of cut-out paper motifs stuck onto a surface to create an ornamental effect.

Dentil A relief moulding for frames, comprising a band of small cubes.

Delineavit or **Del** Latin, meaning "drew it", often seen on prints to indicate the artist's name.

Dry mounting Technique used to attach a work of art to a backing board, which involves inserting a thin sheet of tissue impregnated with glue between the picture and the backing. The glue is then activated by applying heat and pressure.

Drypoint Type of printing where the image is scratched into the metal plate using a sharply pointed implement.

Edition The total number of authorized prints published.

Editioning The printing of the approved edition, distinct from preliminary proofs.

Elevation A flat vertical view of a building or other object.

Embossed A raised surface that stands proud of the paper, formed by engraving and other intaglio techniques.

Engraving Prints made by drawing the image on a metal plate using a tool called a burin or a graver, which extracts V-shaped slivers of metals as the image is drawn.

Epreuve d'artiste or **EA** French term for artist's proof.

Etching Type of printing where an image is drawn onto a metal plate covered in wax. The plate is submerged into a bath of acid that eats into the surface of the plate creating uneven, scratchy lines.

Ex coll (Latin) From the collection, often seen in catalogue descriptions, indicating the provenance of a work of art.

Execudit (Latin) Published it, indicates the name of the publisher, as distinct from the artist and engraver.

Fecit (Latin) Made it, indicates the name of the engraver of a print, as distinct from the artist or publisher.

Foul bite In etching, a term used when the acid causes the acid resistant ground to collapse unintentionally. Gives a granular appearance to the surface of an etching.

Foxing Brownish stains often seen on works on paper caused by mould and exposure to damp air.

Frontispiece Illustration at the front of a book usually facing the title page.

Fugitive colour Fading of pigments caused by exposure to sunlight.

Genre Scene of everyday domestic life or anecdotal subject.

Grisaille French term derived from the word *gris* (grey), which refers to a work painted in monochrome tones.

Ground The preparatory acid-resistant layer applied to a plate before it is etched. The ground is usually made of bitumen, wax and resin and often blackened to show the metal underneath when the artist creates a design.

Guilloche Decorative border formed from interlacing S-curved lines.

Gum Arabic A binding medium used in watercolours to help the pigment to stick to the paper, it is sometimes applied as a solution to hand-coloured prints to give a richer tone.

Hors Commerce or **HC** (French) Indicates prints issued in addition to the main edition, but not for sale, usually for the publisher.

Impression A print made from a plate, stone or wood block.

Inscription Writing on a work of art which is not a signature or a date.

Intaglio printing A printing method which involves incising or cutting an image into the surface of a plate (see p22): aquatints, drypoints, engravings, etchings and mezzotints are all varieties of intaglio printing.

Invenit or **inv** (Latin) Designed by, indicates the painter or designer.

Japan (or Japanese paper) Soft, strong tissue paper made in the Far East and used for mounting and as an artist's paper, especially for prints.

Laid paper Early hand-made paper usually made from linen or rags that has distinctive, close horizontal parallel lines crossed by occasional regularly spaced perpendicular lines.

Line block, Line cut, Line engraving, Line etching Commercial prints made by photomechanical processes.

Lino cut Printing method, similar to woodcut, in which the background is cut away leaving the image in relief.

Lithography Printing method based on the antipathy between grease and water. An image drawn on a flat surface (originally limestone) in a greasy medium, the surface is dampened, and then inked. Ink only sticks to the image, since it is repelled by the water on the rest of the surface and the image can then be printed (see p38).

Margin The plain border area surrounding a print.

Mezzotint Tonal printing method made by roughening a metal plate and smoothing it down to create lighter gradations of tone (see p32).

Mixed method Print made with a combination of two or more techniques.

Monochrome Work of art in varying shades of a single colour.

Monogram Usually the artist's initials, used instead of a signature.

Monotype or **Monoprint** Print made by painting on a sheet of metal or glass and printing by placing a sheet of paper over it. Further impressions are weaker unless the plate is repainted.

Mordant The acid used to bite into a metal plate during the printing process.

Mount Stiff paper board used to protect prints and form a barrier between the glass and the backboard.

Multiple editions More than one edition of the same image. Often different editions were made on paper of different quality and size, larger editions usually on less costly paper.

Oil sketch Work in oils made as a preparation for another work.

Oleograph A colour lithograph varnished and impressed with a grainy texture to simulate an oil painting.

Pinxit (Latin) Painted it, indicates the artist of the original work of art from which the print was made.

Photogravure Intaglio prints made by a commercial photographic process.

Platemark Line made around the edge of a print caused by the pressure of the plate onto the paper.

Photo-mechanical Term used for reproductive prints made using photographic methods.

Pochoir (French) Hand-coloured stencils cut from zinc, popular in the 19th and 20th centuries. Sometimes used combined with printed designs.

Poupée (French) Fabric wadding used to colour a plate or block by hand before printing.

Printer's proof A print made for the printer, in addition to the main edition.

Proof A term for a trial impression taken before the main edition.

Putto Plump angelic child. *Putti* are also sometimes called *amorini*; a cherub is similar but usually has wings.

Provenance The origins and history of a work of art including its past owners.

Recto Front or most extensively worked side of a sheet of paper, or the right-hand page of a book; often used in conjunction with **verso**, meaning the opposite side.

Register mark Small marks found in the margin of a print (often a cross) used to line up a print when different colours are printed.

Relief Decoration which protrudes outwards from the surface.

Retouching Either corrections made by the artist, or more commonly, painting done by a restorer to replace lost and damaged areas and restore a picture to its original state.

Rocker Serrated tool used in the mezzotint process to roughen the surface of the plate.

Roulette Wheeled printer's tool used in the production of mezzotints and other printing processes.

Sanguine Reddish coloured chalk popular for drawing from the 16th century onwards. Stipple engravings and crayon manner etchings were sometimes printed in sepia ink to simulate their effect.

Screenprinting Modern printing technique in which a printed image is made by passing ink through a screen attached to a stencil onto paper (see p46).

Sepia Brown pigment traditionally made from the ink of a squid or octopus, also incorrectly used as a generic term for all brownish ink.

Serigraph US term for screen print.

Signed in the plate Printed signature of the artist within the image. Some prints are signed in the plate and by hand in the margin.

Silkscreen Another term for screen print.

Soft-ground etching Printing method resembling a crayon or chalk drawing in which the etcher draws onto a paper placed on a plate prepared with a sticky ground. When the paper is removed the ground sticks unevenly to the drawn lines, the plate is then etched in a bath of acid before being printed.

States The various stages of a plate, while an engraver is altering a design.

Stipple engraving Printing process in which gradations of tone are made from tiny engraved or etched dots.

Stopping out In etching the use of acid-resistant substances to protect certain areas of the design before reimmersing the plate in the acid.

Sugar lift Modern development of aquatint where the design is painted onto a plate using a mixture of ink and sugar. The plate is coated with varnish and immersed in water which dissolves the sugar/ink leaving the design to be etched in acid and printed; sometimes used in conjunction with aquatint.

Trial proof A preparatory print made before the main edition.

Trompe l'oeil (French) A term meaning to "deceive the eye", used to describe a painting of such great realism that the objects depicted look real.

Tusche liquid Lithographic ink.

Unlimited edition Unsigned prints made in an unnumbered edition.

Verso The back of a sheet of drawings or paintings, or the left hand page of an open book, often used in conjunction with **recto** meaning the opposite.

Vignette Small design or illustration with no strictly defined border.

Wash Broad layers of thin, transparent colour or diluted ink.

Watermarks Marks in the fabric of the paper, visible if the paper is held to the light, used by paper manufacturers as a method of identification.

Woodcut Relief printing technique in which the image is drawn onto a plank, cut parallel to the grain and the background areas cut away (see p16).

Wood engraving Type of woodcut in which a hard wood is cut across the grain and the background is cut away with a tool such as a burin (see p18).

Wove paper Paper made on a fine mesh screen so that the texture is uniform and there is no distinctive grid effect as with laid paper.

INDEX

Page numbers in **bold** type refer to main entries. *Italic* numbers refer to the illustrations

Acknowledgments

Special thanks to Christopher Johnston of Bonham's for all his help.
Special thanks also to the MA Printmaking department, Camberwell College of Arts,The London Institute for their invaluable help in allowing us to photograph printmaking for pp10–13 at the College. The printmakers are Jillian Booth, Antony Carlton and Kirk M. Delstanche.

PHOTOGRAPHIC CREDITS

The publishers would like to thank the copyright holders for their kind permission to reproduce the works on the pages listed below:

Front jacket: tc By permission of the Henry Moore Foundation
Back jacket: tcr The Frink Estate

6 The Estate of Eric Gill; 14 The Estate of George Claude Leon Underwood; 18 rBy permission of the Paul Nash Trustees; 19 l&rThe Estate of Douglas Percy Bliss; 20 rBy Courtesy of EB Power and The Redfern Gallery, London; 21 rBy Courtesy of The Estate of Sybil Andrews and The Redfern Gallery, London; 29 cThe Estate of Sir Frank Brangwyn; 30 tl&li©DACS 1997, rBy Courtesy of EB Power and The Redfern Gallery, London; 38 lThe Frink Estate, 43 Terry Frost; 47 l© Patrick Caulfield 1997 All rights reserved DACS, rAlbert Irvin; 59 rThe Estate of Sir Frank Brangwyn; 84 The Frink Estate; 85 lThe Executors of the Estate of John Piper, rSuccession of H Matisse/DACS 1997; 86 l©ADAGP Paris, and DACS, London 1997, c&rSuccession Picasso/DACS 1997; 87 tl&blSuccession H Matisse/DACS 1997, r©ADAGP, Paris and DACS, London 1997; 88 l©David Hockney, 1980, tr© David Hockey, 1971, brThe Executors of the Estate of John Piper; 89 trElizabeth V Blackadder, l&brBy permission of the Henry Moore Foundation; 90 bl Albert Irvin, rThe Frink Estate; 91 tlVictor Pasmore, blHoward Hodgkin, 96 l&r©ADAGP Paris, and DACS, London 1997; 97 r©ADAGP, Paris and DACS, London 1997; 98 l©DACS 1997; 99 tl,c&r© ADAGP, Paris and DACS, London 1997; 107 l©ADAGP Paris, and DACS, London 1997; 108 tr&br©ADAGP, Paris and DACS, London 1997; 109 lThe Estate of Christopher Richard Wynne Nevinson, r©ADAGP, Paris and DACS, London 1997; 110 ©ADAGP, Paris and DACS, London 1997; 111 Cuneo Fine Art/National Railway Museum/Science & Society Picture Library; 114 lLondon Transport Museum/© Man Ray Trust/ADAGP, Paris and DACS, London 1997, c&rLondon Transport Museum; 115 l&rLondon Transport Museum; 120 rNational Railway Museum/Science & Society Picture Library; 121 r©DACS 1997; 122 t&bShell Art Collection, National Motor Museum Trust, Beaulieu; 123 t,l&r Shell Art Collection, National Motor Museum Trust, Beaulieu; 124 tShell Art Collection, National Motor Museum Trust, Beaulieu, bLondon Transport Museum; 125 London Transport Museum; 126 l,tr&br© IOC/Olympic Museum Collections; 127 l&r©IOC/Olympic Museum Collections; 128 tr&br©DACS 1997; 131 r©ADAGP, Paris and DACS, London 1997; 133 l&br©ADAGP, Paris and DACS, London 1997; 135 Orangina; 137 tl©ADAGP, Paris and DACS, London 1997, bl©DACS 1997; 139 rOz Publications/ Martin Sharp; 144 lFamily Dog Productions; 144 rMartin Sharp; 145 lBill Graham, cHapshash and The Coloured Coat, rGriffin.

LIST OF SOURCES

The publishers would like to thank all those who supplied photographs for use in this book, especially Christie's South Kensington.

Front jacket: tl CSK, tc RIB/IB/CW, tr RIB/KA, bl CSK, bcl CSK, bcr CI, br CI.
Spine: CI.
Back jacket: tl RIB/IB, tcr RIB/IB/CW, tr RIB/KA, bl CI, bcl CSK, bcr CSK, br CSK

8/9 CSK; 10/11 RIB/TR; 12/13 RIB/TR; 14 RIB/IB; 15 CSK; 16 lRIB/IB, rCSK; 17 lSNY, rRIB/IB; 18 l&rCSK; 19 l&r RIB/IB; 20 l&rCSK; 21 l&rCSK; 22 RIB/KA; 23 tl&bl CSK, trRIB/KA; 24 lRIB/IB, tr&riRIB/KA; 25 lCSK, rRIB/IB; 26 lCSK, c&rRIB/KA; 27 l&rCSK; 28 l&rRIB/KA; 29 tlRIB/KA, c& trCSK; 30 tl&liRIB/KA, rCSK; 31 lCSK, rCL; 32 l&r CSK; 33 lRIB/KA, c&rCSK; 34 lCSK, r&ri RIB/KA; 35 lCSK, rRIB/KA; 36 RIB/IB; 37 RIB/KA; 38 l&rRIB/IB; 39 l&rRIB/IB; 40 l&rRIB/IB; 41 lRIB/IB, rRIB/KA; 42 RIB/IB; 43 RIB/IB; 44 RIB/IB; 45 l&rRIB/IB; 46 CSK; 47 lRIB/KA, rRIB/IB; 48 CSK; 49 RIB/KA; 50 lRIB/KA, tr&br O'SG; 51 tl,r&blCSK; 52 l&rRIB/IB, tcCSK; 53 lCSK, cRIB/KA, rRIB/IB; 54/55 RIB/KA; 55 cRIB/IB, trRIB/KA; 56 lRIB/IB, rCSK; 57 lCSK, rRIB/IB; 58 tlSL, bl CSK, rRIB/IB; 59 lCSK, rRIB/IB; 60 tl&bRIB/IB; 60/61 RIB/IB; 61 rCSK, bRIB/IB; 62 l&rRIB/KA; 63 tl,r&bRIB/KA; 64 RIB/KA; 65 RIB/IB; 66 lRIB/IB, rRIB/KA; 67 lRIB/IB, tr&brRIB/ KA; 68 tCSK, bl&br RIB/KA; 69 CSK; 70 l&rRIB/IB; 71 tl&blRIB/IB, rCSK; 72 CSK; 73 l&rRIB/IB; 74 lRIB/KA, rCSK; 75 lRIB/IB, c&rCSK; 76 lRIB/IB, rRIB/KA; 77 lRIB/KA, c&rRIB/IB; 78 RIB/IB; 79 lRIB/IB, c&rCSK; 80 l&trRIB/IB, brCL; 81 l&cRIB/KA, rCSK; 82 l&rRIB/IB; 83 lCSK, tr&brRIB /IB; 84 RIB/IB/CW; 85 lRIB/IB/CW, rRIB/IB/ CW; 86 lRIB/IB/CW, cWO/JRS, rRIB/IB/CW; 87 tl&bl RIB/IB/CW, rRIB/IB/CW; 88 l&trRIB/IB/CW, brRIB/IB/CW; 89 l,tr&brRIB /IB/CW; 90 tlRIB/IB/CW, blRIB/IB/CW, rRIB/IB /CW; 91 tl&blRIB/IB/CW, rCI; 94 CSK; 95 l&rCSK; 96 l,c&rCSK; 97 l&rCSK; 98 l&rCSK; 99 tl,c&rCSK; 100 l&rCSK; 101 l&rCSK; 102 l&cCSK; 102/103 CSK; 103 rCSK; 104 l&rCSK; 105 CSK; 106 CSK; 107 l&rCSK; 108 l,tr&brCSK; 109 l&rCSK; 110 CSK; 111 CSK; 112 tl,bl&rCSK; 113 l&rCSK; 114 l,c&rCSK; 115 l&rCSK; 116 l&rCSK; 117 tl,bl&rCSK; 118 CSK; 119 l&rCSK; 120 l&rCSK; 121 l&rCSK; 122 t&bCSK; 123 t,l&r CSK; 124 t&bCSK; 125 CSK; 126 l,tr&brCSK; 127 l&rCSK; 128 l,tr&brCSK; 129 CSK; 130 CSK; 131 l&rCSK; 132 CSK; 133 l,tc&brCSK; 134 CSK; 135 CI; 136 CSK; 137 tl,bl&rCSK; 138 SL/NM; 139 lSL; 139 rSL/NM; 140 l&rCI; 140/141 CI; 141 CI; 142 l&rSL/NM; 143 l&rSL/NM; 144 lSL/NM, 144 rSL/NM; 145 l,c&rSL/NM; 146 RIB/KA; 147 CSK.

KEY

b *bottom*, c *centre*, i *inset*, l *left*, r *right*, t *top*

CI *Christie's Images*
CL *Christie's London*
CSK *Christie's South Kensington*
CW *Caroline Wiseman*
IB *Ian Booth*
JRS *John R Simmons*
KA *Ken Adlard*
NM *Nigel Mentzel*
O'SG *O'Shea Gallery*
RIB *Reed International Books Ltd*
TR Tim Ridley
SL *Sotheby's London*
SNY *Sotheby's New York*
WO *Wiseman Originals Ltd*